# OUTDOOR ADVENTURE
## MANUAL

Essential Scouting skills for the Great Outdoors

First published in April 2013

A catalogue record for this book is available from the British Library

ISBN 978 0 85733 282 0

Library of Congress control no. 2012948693

Haynes Publishing,
Sparkford, Yeovil, Somerset BA22 7JJ, UK
Tel: +44 (0) 1963 442030
Fax: +44 (0) 1963 440001
E-mail: sales@haynes.co.uk
Website: www.haynes.co.uk

Haynes North America, Inc.,
861 Lawrence Drive, Newbury Park,
California 91320, USA

Printed in the USA by Odcombe Press LP,
1299 Bridgestone Parkway, La Vergne, TN 37086

Compiled and edited by Chris James
Special editorial consultants:
    Austin Lill and Terry Longhurst
Staged photography by Tudor Morgan-Owen
Cover photo by Chloe Chapman, taken at Hawkhirst
    Scout Activity Centre **www.scouts.org.uk/sac**
Photo of Bear Grylls:
    Martyn Milner/The Scout Association
Designed by Richard Parsons

## WARNING!

# CONTENTS

# FOREWORD
# BY BEAR GRYLLS

You'll probably know that I spend a lot of time outdoors. Whether this is in Antarctica, the Himalayas, or just on the deck of my houseboat with my children, I always find that something special happens when I step out into the open.

I feel not only energised, but also a powerful sense of belonging – as if this is where we should really be. In the wild, almost everything you see is alive, and this powerful life force runs through everything, including ourselves. Nature's presence is very strong.

We have a lot to learn from Nature: its quiet strength in adversity; its instinctive sense of renewal and stoicism. The philosopher Lao Tzu said: 'Nature does not hurry, yet everything is accomplished.' How often do you find yourself rushing about, only to find you've accomplished nothing at all? The trick is to act only when you need to and keep growing.

Scouting provides the perfect place for people to grow – and that includes adults and young people, and we never stop learning from each other.

When it comes to outdoor skills, Scouting is so full of knowledge. Over 100 years the most amazing skills have been passed on from leader to leader, Scout to Scout or mother and father to son and daughter, but it rarely gets written down. Until now. We've tracked down our best outdoors people and managed to get them to stand still long enough to scribble down their secrets – from how to rig a hammock and tarpaulin, to making rope from nettle stalks (yes, you did read that right).

Despite the brilliant ideas you'll find in this book, there's still no substitute for learning from a real person. So if you enjoy what you read, and are enthusiastic about all things outdoors, why not seek out your local Scout Group and let one of our volunteers (or brilliant young people) show you the ropes? We need people like you.

And if you're put off by the cold and rain, then remember this little quote from Alice Te Miha: 'No sky is heavy, if the heart be light.'

**Bear Grylls**
Chief Scout

# THE GREAT OUTDOORS

From Bill Shakespeare to Bill Bryson, writers and poets have celebrated our fields and mountains, rivers and valleys. The Great Outdoors has the power to lift our spirits and raise our aspirations. As the Bard said: 'One touch of nature makes the whole world kin.' Whether whitewater rafting or rambling in the hills, the outdoors is there for all of us to enjoy at our own pace and in our own way.

# THE GREAT OUTDOORS
## A BRIEF HISTORY

The Great Outdoors, of course, has always been with us, but we have only perceived it in the modern sense as a place for camping and leisure activities over the past 100 years.

### The Great Outdoors

'I love the Great Outdoors,' a Scout once said. 'Except when it rains, in which case it's just the outdoors'.

This book is all about making the most of our extraordinary natural world, and in all sorts of weather. For over 100 years Scouts have been camping, hiking, climbing and canoeing in the Great Outdoors. This has given us unparalleled knowledge of how to operate safely in these environments, and we've amassed thousands of skills and tips that make outdoor life easier. Whether you're planning a family outing to the Cotswolds, or a month in Borneo, you can use this book to ensure you're always prepared.

How often have you looked through the car window, beyond the hedgerows and into the fields beyond? Perhaps you've wondered what kind of trees you can see, or what lies beyond the next hill. There's something deep down in all of us that's drawn to the countryside – and it's probably worth remembering that until very recently almost all people lived in rural communities. The outdoors reconnects us with a natural state, a simpler time; it reminds us that beyond our sophistication, computers, gadgets and fashions we're animals after all.

The health benefits of spending quality time outdoors are well documented. According to a recent study, patients are proven to recover more quickly when they have natural views of trees and grass. Something as simple as a walk in the country can relieve stress, depression, reduce blood pressure and cut the risk of heart disease. Outdoor exercise is routinely prescribed by doctors as the best medicine (second only to laughter). It was Jane Austen who said: 'to sit in the shade on a fine day and look upon verdure [greenery] is the most perfect refreshment.'

In children, the benefits are even more pronounced. Any parent will tell you that an afternoon running about in the local country park results in their children getting a better night's sleep. Outdoor exercise improves concentration. Physical activity, especially playing games, helps promote teamwork, hand-eye co-ordination and social skills. Children naturally devise games and assign roles when left to play together outside. It's no surprise therefore that Robert Baden-Powell, the Founder of Scouting, put the outdoors at the very heart of his scheme for young people. 'The open air is the real objective of Scouting,' he remarked, 'and the key to its success.'

While the range of activities Scouting offers may have expanded to include such improbable things as zorbing and paragliding, the simple principle behind Scouting remains unchanged. We encourage people to get outside, make friends and create their own adventures.

## The first campsite

If we're to discount the Roman praetorium, the type of campsite used by the original Italian visitors to Great Britain, the first modern incarnation of a campsite was Cunningham Camp in Howstrake on the Isle of Man in 1894. Perhaps understandably, given the social mores of the time, it was originally only for men. With 600 visitors each week, however, it was a sign that camping for fun was here to stay.

Native Americans revere Nature as a higher power. 'Man's heart away from nature becomes hard,' says Standing Bear. 'There is a correlation between the natural rhythms of life and our own natural rhythms. If we separate ourselves from nature, we are disconnecting ourselves from everything that gives us life and purpose'. The practice of bushcraft has seen a revival recently, with many Western trackers turning to ancient cultures and tribes to learn the forgotten skills of tracking, foraging and fire-lighting used by our distant ancestors.

The hippy notion of 'heading to the country' and reconnecting with nature has entered the mainstream and is still seen as the perfect antidote to stressful, impersonal city living. Many aspire to have a second home in an idyllic rural location or by the coast. It embodies our dreams of freedom and escape.

The truth is that you don't need a second home to enjoy the countryside. You can pick up a tent for two people as cheaply as the price of a couple of pints. It might not have a colour TV, but it will at least be a roof over your head.

In Scouting, camping is actually growing in popularity. Sales of our Nights Away badges – earned by young people for spending a night away from home, more often than not under canvas – increase annually. Among the general public camping is also on the increase, with the advent of the 'staycation' – the low-cost domestic holiday.

# WHO INVENTED CAMPING?

The idea of spending time outdoors as a recreation came about some time during the Industrial Revolution and gained real popularity at the start of the 20th century. The year 1908 was big for camping. Not only did it see the publication of Baden-Powell's *Scouting for Boys*, the classic 'instructor' in the art of camping and good citizenship, but also the first *Campers' Handbook*. Written by Thomas Hiram Holding, a travelling tailor, this was one of the key texts that popularised camping for leisure among the general public. Both Baden-Powell and Holding could lay claim to being the founding fathers of the Great Outdoors.

While these two books fought it out in the bestseller charts, hundreds of thousands of Scouts were enjoying their first adventures, breaking out of the grim inner cities and into the countryside. Meanwhile, the Great British public was also catching the camping bug, with the keenest members coalescing into the Camping Club of Great Britain and Ireland. Proving his growing significance in all matters camping, Baden-Powell became its president alongside his other, perhaps more famous, role as Chief Scout.

# OVER 100 YEARS OF ADVENTURE

Scouting began outdoors, of course, with a camp on Brownsea Island, in Poole Harbour in August 1907. Choosing 22 boys from a variety of backgrounds, Robert Baden-Powell organised eight days of activities on this picturesque island, among red squirrels and peacocks.

## The first Scout camps

Robert Baden-Powell's aim with his camp on Brownsea Island was to try out his new ideas. At this stage he hadn't envisaged a movement – merely a programme of activities that other organisations, such as the Boys' Brigade, could use.

The camp was a great success, with the group learning everything from fire-lighting to sailing. Baden-Powell then retired to the windmill on Wimbledon Common to write up his ideas in what would become one of the biggest-selling books of the 20th century: *Scouting for Boys*.

Tens of thousands of youngsters bought the book – first in its series of eight parts, and many more as a complete book – and started forming themselves into troops. The first official Scout camp took place at Humshaugh, Northumberland between 22 August and 4 September 1908, based on the techniques developed at Brownsea.

In order to provide national support and leadership, Baden-Powell opened the Boy Scouts Association offices at 116 Victoria Street, London, in May 1909. Following another experimental camp held on board the training ship *Mercury*, the Sea Scouts branch was formed in October 1910, based on *Sea Scouting for Boys* by B-P's eldest brother, Warrington Baden-Powell.

The Crystal Palace Rally held in 1909 and media coverage of female Scouts mixing with boys led to the creation of the Girl Guides Movement, but it would be another 80 years before the Association became co-educational. In recognition of its achievements and status, a Royal Charter was granted to the Association on 4 January 1912 by King George V.

## The movement grows

By the beginning of 1914 an experimental scheme for Wolf Cubs had been created to cater for children too young to become Scouts; two years later the scheme became a formal section, largely based on the experiences and writings of Miss Vera Barclay. The same year saw the first National Good Turn, which involved Scouts assisting the blind. Scouting also offered opportunities for those with disabilities, be they physical or mental, to benefit from the same skills and experience by forming troops in specialist schools and hospitals.

The First World War involved Scouts taking part in messenger duties on the home front, fundraising for ambulances and running recreation huts for troops behind the front lines. In 1917 another section was created, for those over 18 who wanted to continue Scouting without becoming adult leaders: initially named Senior Scouts, a year later they were renamed Rover Scouts.

The war led to the loss of many Scouts between 1914 and 1918, such as Jack Cornwell VC, a 16-year-old boy who died during the Battle of Jutland and was awarded the highest military decoration for courage under fire. In recognition of Cornwell's heroism the Association created the Cornwell Badge for Scouts who have suffered severe ailments and this is still awarded to this day. Many thousands of Scout leaders were also killed in the war, which prevented many Troops from reforming after it ended but also led Baden-Powell to start international Jamborees to bring together the youth of the world.

## A home for Scouting

The years following the war saw many key developments that would remain part of Scouting to the present day. Thanks to the generosity of Mr de Bois Maclaren, Gilwell Park was purchased. This facility was to provide adult leader training, with the added benefit of being within walking distance of the East End, enabling Scouts from urban London to experience the countryside. In September 1919 the first adult training course took place, known as the Wood Badge. Those who completed the course were entitled to wear two wooden beads and the Gilwell scarf, which included a piece of Maclaren tartan in memory of Gilwell Park's benefactor. Two years after that first course a reunion was held for all those who'd completed Wood Badge training and this remains an annual event at Gilwell Park, bringing together those in Scouting from around the world.

## Chief Scout of the World

Robert Baden-Powell wrote no fewer than 32 books, the earnings from which helped to pay for his Scouting travels. As with all his successors, he received no salary as Chief Scout. He received various honorary degrees and the freedom of a number of cities, along with 28 foreign orders and decorations and 19 foreign Scout awards.

In 1938, suffering ill-health, B-P went to Africa to live in semi-retirement in Nyeri, Kenya, where he died on 8 January 1941 at the age of 83. He is buried in a simple grave at Nyeri within sight of Mount Kenya. On his headstone are the words: 'Robert Baden-Powell, Chief Scout of the World', alongside Scout and Guide emblems. He was later commemorated in Westminster Abbey, London.

B-P is remembered on Founder's Day, celebrated each year on his birthday, 22 February. To this day Scouts continue to enjoy activities in the outdoors and live out his ideas. As the great man once said, 'life without adventure would be deadly dull'.

## A global gathering

The first World Scout Jamboree was staged at Olympia in London during July and August 1920, enabling each country's Scouts to introduce their culture to each other. It was also at Olympia that Baden-Powell was declared Chief Scout of the World. The Group system was introduced in 1928, which allowed different sections such as Wolf Cub Packs, Scout Troops, Rover Crews and Sea Scouts to operate under one organisation.

Scouting not only promoted service to others and outdoor skills, but through various initiatives also provided opportunities for those with creative talents to flourish. This included the Scout Musical Festival, first staged in 1924 at the Royal College of Music, and the London Gang Show in 1934, both of which allowed Scouts to compose music and create theatrical sketches and perform them at prestigious venues. There was also the Scout Car Races, which began as the Soap Box Derby held at the Brooklands circuit in 1939. This competition allowed Scouts to design and construct their own pedal-powered vehicles, gaining knowledge of aerodynamics and mechanics on a limited budget. These diverse opportunities have led to a varied alumni of Scouting, including Sir Stirling Moss and Sir Paul McCartney. The 1930s also saw the introduction of the Handicapped Scouts Branch in 1936, which had evolved during the movement's earliest days to provide Scouting to those with disabilities.

# THE ORIGINAL OUTDOORSMAN

Like many brilliant people, Robert Baden-Powell failed plenty of examinations. He preferred the outdoors to the classroom and spent much of his time sketching wildlife in the woods around his school. His irrepressible personality infuriated and charmed his teachers at Charterhouse School in equal measure.

Robert Stephenson Smyth Baden-Powell, or B-P (or 'Stephe' as he was known as a child), was born in Paddington, London, on 22 February 1857. He was the eighth of ten children of the Reverend Baden-Powell, a professor at Oxford University.

During the holidays, he and his brothers were always in search of adventure. One vacation was spent on a yachting expedition around the south coast of England, while on another they traced the Thames to its source by canoe.

After school Baden-Powell went into the army, where he led a distinguished career through postings in countries including India, Afghanistan, Malta and various parts of Africa. His most famous achievement was the defence of Mafeking against the Boers in 1899, after which he became a Major-General at the age of only 43.

Baden-Powell retired from the Army in 1910 at the age of 53, on the advice of King Edward VII, who suggested B-P could do more valuable service for his country working on developing Scouting and its sister movement, Guiding.

In 1912 he married Olave Soames, by whom he had three children (Peter, Heather and Betty). At the Third World Scout Jamboree, the Prince of Wales announced that B-P had been created a peer. He took the title of Lord Baden-Powell of Gilwell.

The Second World War brought challenges and innovation to the Association in equal measure. Lord Baden-Powell died on 8 January 1941, to be replaced as Chief Scout by Lord Somers a few months later; tghen Lord Somers died in May 1944 and was succeeded by Lord Rowallan in April 1945. In terms of innovation, the Air Scout branch was launched in January 1941 and held their first National Air Scout Camp and Exhibition a year later.

In April 1941 a commission was set up to consider post-war developments and it produced *The Road Ahead* report in September 1945. This recommended how Scouting needed to adapt in order to address the changes in society that had occurred since 1908. Scout International Relief Service Teams were created and embedded within the British Army to provide care and support to children and the survivors of the concentration camps in liberated Europe.

The post-war years saw the introduction of the Senior Scout Section and a new programme for Rover Scouts in 1946, and the creation of the B-P Guild of Old Scouts in 1948. The first 'Bob-a-Job' Week occurred in April 1949 and proved to be an inspired initiative, mixing community work with raising funds for the Association and local Groups.

The Air Scout programme was also progressing, with the first gliding course for Scouts at Lasham in July 1955. Sir Charles Maclean took over from Lord Rowallan as Chief Scout. The 1960s ushered in many changes starting with the opening of Baden-Powell House in London by the Queen in July 1961. This was built as a memorial to the Founder, a meeting place and a hostel for Scouts from around the world, and the facility

continues to this day, just across from the Natural History Museum. At the same time the Soap Box Derby was renamed the National Scoutcar Races. The creative side of Scouting wasn't ignored either with the first National Scout Band Championships in May 1965 and the start of the Scout and Guide National 'Folk Fest' in June 1968.

The most dramatic changes came from the Chief Scout's Advance Party Report published in June 1966. This led to a new Promise and Law, changes in the uniform to introduce long trousers and berets as standard, new training schemes for the Cub Scouts, Scouts and Venture Scouts, with minimum standards relating to Group strength and progress in training. Three National Scout Activity Centres were created at Lasham, Longridge and Whernside in March 1968, and the first National Family Camp took place at Gilwell Park in May 1969.

Ahead of decimalisation 'Bob-a-Job' week was renamed Scout Job Week in 1970. The World Membership Badge was introduced in 1971 to illustrate global solidarity in Scouting. Later that year Lord Maclean stepped down as Chief Scout and in the following year Sir William Gladstone was appointed. Ralph Reader presented the final London Gang Show at the Gaumont State Theatre in 1974 due to retirement from writing and producing. The Association's Headquarters moved from Buckingham Palace Road to Baden-Powell House in the same year.

Also during the 1970s a fundraising drive made enough money to commission an RNLI lifeboat called *The Scout*, which entered service at Hartlepool in 1977. Girls became eligible for Venture Scouts in July 1976, and 15 years later the Royal Charter was amended to make the Association fully co-educational. The start of 1979 saw the launch of 'Cub Country' to aid community projects in Nepal during the International Year of the Child.

The 1980s reflected the economic changes taking place in the UK, with the National Air Activities Centre at Lasham closing in March 1980 and the introduction of the 'Scouting and Unemployment' scheme. In 1982 the 75th anniversary of the Brownsea Island Experimental Camp was celebrated as the Year of the Scout, with a launch at the House of Commons. The year also saw the retirement of Sir William Gladstone and the appointment of Major-General Michael Walsh as Chief Scout. Extoree '82 brought together 1,500 handicapped and able-bodied Scouts for an international camp at Gilwell Park. The same year also saw the start of Beaver Scouts for boys between the ages of six and eight. Five hundred Venture Scouts assisted with the St John Ambulance Centenary Party in Hyde Park and at the same event broke a world record by cooking a nine-mile-long sausage. After six years Major-General Michael Walsh retired as Chief Scout and was replaced by Mr Garth Morrison. The Venture Scout Section celebrated its 21st birthday with 'Everest' climbs in cities throughout the country, with Sir Edmund Hillary attending in London. The Scout Athlete Badge became the first proficiency

badge to be commercially sponsored, by the 'Matchstick' sportswear brand in 1989. That year also saw the decision to abolish all headwear, while the Scout Leadership Training Programme received a commendation from the Department of Employment.

Scouting's care for the environment was also recognised with the launch of the 'Green Charter' Competition in 1990 and the hosting of 170 children from the Chernobyl area for a holiday in 1991. The first national fundraising appeal since 1938 was launched as the 'Promise Appeal', which went on to raise £2.5 million by 1992. The Scout and Cub Scout Laws were revised slightly as a result of the Association becoming fully co-educational.

Mr George Purdy was appointed Chief Scout in 1996, and the same year the Association website was launched along with the Pilot Scout Network scheme. Initiatives such as the Equal Opportunities Policy, 1996, and a 'Voice for Young People', 1998, were introduced to get people under the age of 25 on national committees.

The new millennium has brought further changes, with the Headquarters moving from Baden-Powell House to a purpose-built office building at Gilwell Park in 2001. Later that year came new uniforms, designed by Meg Andrews, and a new youth programme with revised age ranges in 2002. In 2004 *Blue Peter* action man Peter Duncan was chosen as the new Chief Scout, creating more publicity for the Association. In 2007 the UK hosted the 21st World Scout Jamboree, with 40,000 participants camping at Hylands Park and Brownsea Island, and a live show at the Millennium Dome in London. Lieutenant-Commander Bear Grylls RN became the latest Chief Scout at a handover ceremony on 11 July 2009 at Gilwell Park.

In the 21st century the Scout Association continues to be relevant to society, providing a mix of activities and adventure, life skills and creative energy while providing valuable service to the community.

# ABOUT THIS BOOK

So what can you expect from this book? Quite simply everything Scouting has learnt in its long and eventful history. You'll find out how to make your own table and chairs using little more than sticks and a few well-chosen knots. You'll discover there's more than one way to light a fire. Ray Mears once memorably told a group of Cubs: 'I have two ways of lighting a fire on my person and 40 more in my head.' The Cubs gazed in wonder at his head, as if expecting sparks to fly from his ears.

This is not a survival book, although we do have a chapter on survival skills. You will find other books steeped in the lore of extreme survival. But it does contain the best and most useful skills you'll need when travelling or camping, and everything you need when looking after yourself, your friends, Scouts or family while enjoying the outdoors. When you open a Haynes Manual you should expect simple, easy-to-follow advice, and that's exactly what you'll find here. We've persuaded some of our best Scouting volunteers to share their hard-earned outdoor knowhow in the interests of preserving these valuable skills for the next generation. You'll find hints and tips that will make the outdoors come to life.

# THE WORLD AROUND YOU

From the Cheddar Gorge to the Isle of Mull, the UK, for its relatively small size, is one of the most geographically diverse places in the world. We are a treasure island of mountains, waterfalls, spectacular coastline, caves and lakes. For thrill seekers we're an adventure playground; for nature lovers it's a paradise. Whether you're hiking, canoeing, climbing or walking, it's essential that you're familiar with your surroundings to get the most from your time in the outdoors.

# PREPARING FOR THE GREAT OUTDOORS

Before you set out off on any expedition, always ensure that you have everything that you'll need – you're unlikely to find a corner-shop when you're miles from anywhere!

## Footwear

The first priority is to have a good pair of strong walking boots or shoes. Fashion trainers or boots are useless on rough or wet terrain, and although wellingtons are waterproof they don't provide adequate support for your feet and ankles.

Walking boots or shoes are designed to provide the proper protection and support and to keep your feet comfortable. When you buy them, think about the use you're going to put them to. Low-cut, lightweight boots and shoes without ankle support are meant for easy terrain and summer walking. If you intend to walk all year round and in all sorts of terrain or weather you'll need robust leather or waterproof fabric boots designed for hill walking or trekking. These will support your ankles and feet, and their tough, treaded soles will provide grip on steep, wet ground.

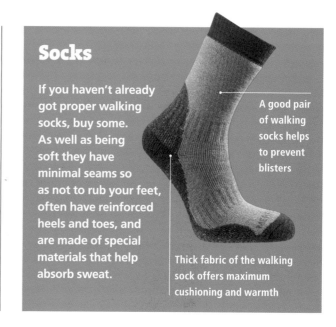

## Socks

If you haven't already got proper walking socks, buy some. As well as being soft they have minimal seams so as not to rub your feet, often have reinforced heels and toes, and are made of special materials that help absorb sweat.

A good pair of walking socks helps to prevent blisters

Thick fabric of the walking sock offers maximum cushioning and warmth

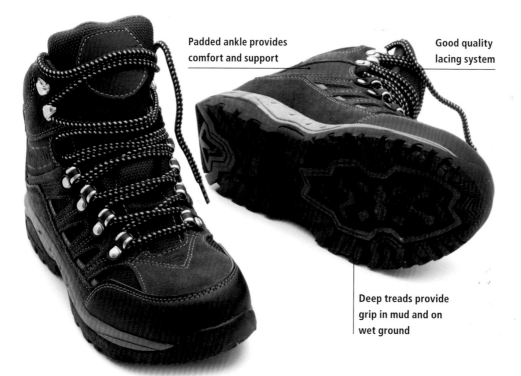

Padded ankle provides comfort and support

Good quality lacing system

Deep treads provide grip in mud and on wet ground

Always try boots out in the shop before you buy them, ideally with the same sort of thick socks that you whould wear outdoors.

After you've bought your boots, always 'break them in' before you head out into the countryside, otherwise you may well suffer from blisters and sores. Wearing them around the house for an hour or so each day during the build-up to your adventure should suffice. Even with these precautions, it is sensible to take plasters or blister pads with you on your hike.

Always keep your boots clean and waterproofed.

# BASIC EQUIPMENT

Time and again people end up in difficulty by being poorly equipped. How much other kit you'll need will depend on the activity, terrain and weather. The basics are as follows:

- Maps and a compass
- A full water bottle
- A thermos of hot drink if the weather's cold
- Snacks, ideally things that can provide a quick energy boost (such as cereal bars, dried fruit, nuts and chocolate, or a sandwich)
- A mobile phone (in a plastic bag to protect it from damp and cold) plus a spare battery for it
- Personal first aid kit (see page 169)
- Sunscreen
- Notepad and pencil
- Plastic bags (to sit on and put rubbish in)
- Wet wipes, or tissues and a small bottle of antiseptic handwash gel

# LONGER EXPEDITIONS

For more ambitious trips it's sensible to pack the following items, most of which are designed to sustain life if you're trapped by weather or injury:

- A whistle to attract attention (the internationally recognised emergency signal is six short blasts, repeated every minute)
- A torch (the internationally recognised emergency signal is six flashes, repeated every minute)
- Wristwatch (as a backup to the clock on your phone)
- Lots of high-calorie nutritious food in case you're out longer than anticipated
- Extra drinking water
- Emergency water purification tablets
- A survival bag (a strong plastic or foil bag big enough to fit over one or two people but able to fold into a compact pouch)
- Alternatively a nylon bothy bag can accommodate several people
- A personal survival kit (see page 174)

# LAYERING UP

Your body temperature will vary depending on the weather and the amount of energy you use. For this reason it's far better to wear several layers of thin, warm clothing that you can easily remove, rather than one thick jacket. Layers of thin clothing trap air between them, providing good insulation without too much weight or bulk. Damp clothing soaks heat from your body, and wind can lower your body temperature even further, creating the danger of hypothermia. Similarly, if you overheat you can suffer from hyperthermia.

# Layering

**Base layer**

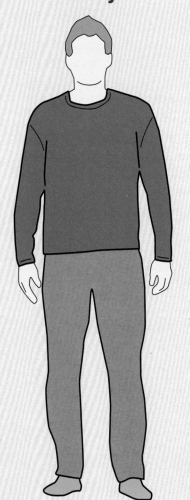

**Mid layer**

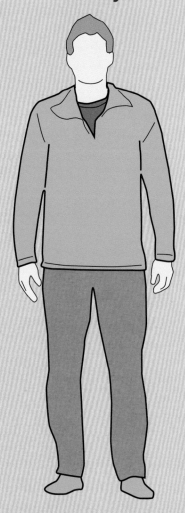

### Base layer
The layer nearest to your skin should be well-fitting but not too tight, perhaps a long-sleeved thermal vest in winter or a sleeveless or short-sleeved top in summer. 'Breathable' synthetic fabrics are preferable to cotton, which gets clammy when you sweat.

### Mid layer
The next layer should be looser, with a high collar and long sleeves that can be rolled up when required – perhaps a warm shirt or polo-neck in winter, or a light shirt in summer.

### Outer layer
If needed, the third layer for extra warmth should be a loose fleece or woollen pullover, preferably one with a zip front. In mild, dry weather this can also act as the final layer (although a waterproof shell that folds up small is always useful).

### Waterproof layer
The final layer, when needed, should be a windproof and waterproof jacket, preferably with a raised collar and a hood. Overlapping fastenings and pocket flaps will help keep the wind out and shed rainwater, while adjustable collar fastenings and underarm vents help to avoid overheating.

## Trousers

On a short easy walk any pair of comfortable, loose-fitting trousers will suffice, but for more arduous walks it's worth getting a pair of proper outdoor trousers made of light synthetic materials that dry quickly. Many have the option of zipping off the lower portion to turn them into shorts. Denim jeans are the worst thing to wear, as they retain water, which will cause chafing and make you cold. Thermal leggings can be worn under trousers in cold weather, or you could wear quilted trousers instead.

In very wet conditions you should wear waterproof trousers over your walking trousers, but always take them off once the rain stops, as they can become very sweaty on the inside.

You might prefer to wear shorts in summer, but remember that these offer little protection from thorns or nettles.

## Hats and gloves

In summer a hat will protect your face, ears and neck from sunburn, and you'll need a good sun cream on every part of your skin that's exposed to the sun. A lightweight hat with a brim will keep the sun out of your eyes. Sunglasses are also useful.

In cold weather a fitted fleece or knitted hat will keep your head and ears warm. When it's very cold a balaclava will also protect your neck and the sides of your face.

To keep your hands warm, fleece or thermal gloves are both warm and light. In very cold conditions you could wear thin gloves underneath heavier mittens. Waterproof gloves are also an option.

**Outer bottom layer**

**Outer top layer**

**Waterproof layer**

# HILLS AND MOUNTAINS

An often hostile, rugged and remote environment, mountains cover 20% of the Earth's land surface. Their quickly changing weather conditions can be treacherous for unprepared walkers.

## Vegetation

Mountainous environments often have clear zones of vegetation due to the complex environmental relationship caused by changes in altitude. At the bottom of the slopes forests can develop, but as you move up the mountainside trees are replaced by heath-land or meadow plants. At the summit the conditions are often so unfavourable that vegetation is mainly restricted to mosses and lichens that have adapted to survive in this environment.

Rhododendron is becoming an increasing issue for those trying to conserve and protect mountain environments in the UK. A particularly robust invasive species, rhododendron can quickly cover vast areas of land and disrupt the already delicate balance of vegetation.

## Mammals

Wild highland animals include the mountain hare, deer, rabbits and foxes. Flocks of hardy sheep are a frequent sight in many mountain areas, while in the Cairngorms there's even a herd of free-roaming reindeer!

## Birds

Mountain birds include golden eagles, buzzards, ravens, crows and twites. The golden eagle is the UK's second largest bird of prey (after the white-tailed eagle), with a wingspan of about 2m. Once almost extinct in Britain, golden eagles are gradually returning to our mountains.

## Erosion of mountain paths

With the increasing popularity of climbing and trekking in mountainous areas, there's growing concern for the integrity of mountain pathways. Many of these are of ancient origin and have been tramped for thousands of years. However, with the advent of large parties taking part in challenge events these have begun to deteriorate rapidly. The combination of a large group of people moving at speed in poor weather is causing rapid and largely avoidable erosion.

As many challenge events take place throughout the year, and especially in wet weather, there's little time for the environment to recover naturally. So think carefully about the size of your group, as well as checking the weather forecast. Quite apart from anything else, climbing as part of a small group in pleasant conditions is a much more agreeable way to enjoy the outdoors!

While enjoying the mountains also think about the noise you make, particularly at night when returning from a climb in high spirits; one of the beauties of our mountains is their serenity.

# UK'S HIGHEST MOUNTAINS

**①  Ben Nevis**
Scotland
1,344m

**②  Snowdon**
Wales
1,085m

**③  Scafell Pike**
England
978m

**④  Slieve Donard**
Northern Ireland
849m

When it comes to discussing the highest mountains in the UK, really we're talking about Scottish mountains. The ten tallest in the UK are all found in Scotland, and are all above 1,200m. Ben Macdui, while being much less famous than its taller brother, Ben Nevis, is just 35m shorter. Climbers are inveterate list-makers and use them to 'bag' peaks, and a few of the categories – with their nicknames – are as follows:

- **Munros** – the 283 Scottish mountains over 3,000ft (914m).
- **Corbetts** – the 221 Scottish mountains between 2,500ft (762m) and 3,000ft (914m) with a drop on all sides of at least 500ft (152m).
- **Grahams** – the 224 Scottish hills between 2,000ft (610m) and 2,500ft (762m) with a drop on all sides of at least 150m (492ft).
- **Donalds** – the 140 hills over 2,000ft (610m) in the Scottish Lowlands.
- **Nuttalls** – the 253 English and 190 Welsh hills over 2,000ft (610m) with a drop on all sides of at least 50ft (15m).
- **Wainwrights** – hills in the Lake District noted by the celebrated walker Alfred Wainwright.
- **Marilyns** – 1,554 hills in England, Wales and Scotland with a drop on all sides of 500ft (152m).

# WOODLANDS AND FORESTS

Forests in the UK were originally designated as places for royalty to hunt deer. Although natural woodlands generally contain a variety of tree species, they're often dominated by either deciduous or coniferous trees.

## Vegetation

In dense woodland there's often very little undergrowth, but in clearings, along paths and rides and in areas of thinner canopy cover, a multitude of plants can be found. Bluebells, violets, wild garlic and primroses are just some of the colourful flowering plants you'll see.

## Mammals

Many animals make their home in our woodlands. Deer and squirrels are a frequent sight in some places, while badgers, foxes and various types of mice and shrew are also present, though harder to see. Rarer forest inhabitants include martens, red squirrels and wild boar.

### Wood mouse

These rodents are found mostly at night in fields, forests and grasslands. They feed mostly on tree seeds, which are taken back to their burrows and nests rather than eaten on the spot. Fruit, berries and even small snails also form part of their diet. They breed between February and October. If you have any trouble telling the difference between a wood mouse and a house mouse, look out for the ears and eyes – they are larger on a wood mouse.

### Stoat

Stoats are surprisingly large, fierce creatures with a reputation for thievery; they'll swipe anything, from mice and rabbits to game and eggs. While usually quiet, which assists their stealthy behaviour, they make a trilling sound before mating, hiss when anxious, and are even known to bark when aggressive. Not to be confused with the smaller weasel.

### Muntjac deer

Found mostly in southern England, the Midlands, East Anglia and South Wales, the Muntjac is small and russet brown. Introduced from China a century ago, they've spread into the wild from private ownership at Woburn Park and are now common. They feed mainly on small shrubs and plants such as brambles, heather and small shoots. Listen out for their distinctive bark. They can be seen mostly at dusk or dawn.

### Squirrel

The now rare red squirrel has been native to Britain for thousands of years. Though, contrary to popular belief, they didn't directly fall victim to the grey squirrel when the latter was introduced from North America in the late 19th century, the grey has proved more adaptable and versatile. Carrying more body fat, which helps it survive harsher winters, the grey squirrel is also quite content to forage on the ground. The more secretive red squirrel prefers the safety of high conifer branches.

Life hasn't been easy for the red squirrel in recent times. Succumbing in large numbers to an outbreak of paraproxvirus in the 1920s, they were also actively hunted for their pelts, but are now protected. They can still be seen in significant numbers on Brownsea Island, Dorset – the birthplace of Scouting – but are otherwise only common in northern Britain and the Isle of Wight. They produce two litters each year, in spring and summer.

### Red deer

This beautiful animal is also the UK's largest land mammal. While famously associated with the Scottish Highlands, they can also be seen in the Lake District, East Anglia and south-west England. Feeding on grass and tree roots, stags can grow up to 190kg, while hinds grow up to 120kg. While browner in colour than their name suggests, their coats are more reddish in summer and greyer in winter.

### Badger

Badgers (from the French becheur, meaning 'digger') are among the UK's most distinctive animals; immediately recognisable from their black and white markings and small heads, they're nocturnal by nature and are more at home underground than above it. While they were once very numerous, there are now only around 300,000 badgers in the UK, two-thirds of them in England. They make their homes in setts (networks of tunnels and chambers) in groups of five or so, on sloping, easy-to-dig soil, often near fields with good drainage. Badgers are omnivores, eating animals and plants, and their diet varies depending on available food, with earthworms as their principle foodstuff, supplemented with fruit and berries, insects, frogs and even birds.

## Stag beetles

Stag beetles are one of the most impressive and distinctive insects scuttling about our woodlands. However, they're now found only in southern and south-west England, and are a protected species. With their antlers (actually mandibles, or jaws), used for eating and warding off rivals, males can grow up to 12cm, although few are larger than 5cm. One of their preferred environments is rotting logs, where the females lay their eggs, and the grubs feed on the rotting wood in the first stages of their development. Males will fight for territorial rights over the most appetising logs!

## Birds

Due to the vast amount of food available in woodlands, bird species are abundant. Nuthatches, jays and crossbills make the most of the available seeds, while woodpeckers, goldcrests and coal tits enjoy the plentiful supply of insects. Tawny owls and goshawks can be found preying on smaller birds and mammals.

# IDENTIFYING TREES

One of the easiest ways to identify a tree is by its leaf shape. In the right season, fruits, nuts, seeds and flowers can also help, while in winter you're generally restricted to looking at the overall shape of the tree and its bark. Here are a few examples of the identifying characteristics of some common British leaves, but for a full range you'll need a tree identification handbook.

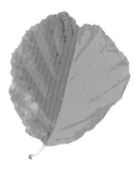

### Alder
Look for the serrated edge; this is alternate and simple, round and without a point – compare with the Hazel leaf.

### Ash
Now threatened by ash dieback disease, the ash can be recognised by its opposite, slender leaves.

### Beech
The beech leaf is entire (no portions missing at the edges). The tree has a dense leaf canopy and soft bark.

### Cherry
Observe the unusually long leaf, used to catch more light – especially where crowded by other trees.

### Elder
Elder leaves appear in opposite pairs, with a single leaf at the end; look out for the serrated edge.

### Field maple
The Canadian flag may help you remember the shape of the field maple leaf – usually with three to five lobes.

### Hazel
Hazel leaves, oval-shaped and pointed at the tip, appear alternately on the stem.

### Holly
Alternate leaves which curve into sharp points; you will also be familiar with the holly tree's clumps of scarlet berries.

### Horse chestnut
With its long-stalked leaves, dividing into up to seven leaflets, the horse chestnut is equally well-known for its conkers.

## Deciduous or coniferous?

Deciduous trees shed their leaves annually, whereas coniferous species remain green throughout the year. Deciduous tree species include oak, ash and beech. Evergreens include Scots pine, yew and holly.

### Birch

Notice the triangular shape of birch leaves, which are alternate on the stem and double-toothed.

### Hawthorn

The Hawthorn can also be recognised by its lobes, which cut deeply into the leaf.

### Oak

Familiar as the emblem of the National Trust, the oak leaf has 'spiral' patterns, accompanied by acorns.

# WOODLAND MANAGEMENT

Over the centuries, various management techniques have left their mark on our woods. Evidence of coppicing and pollarding can be seen on many trees throughout the UK, and is easily recognisable. These techniques are used to harvest poles for fencing, light constructions and firewood, among other things. Cutting back the trees opens up the canopy, allowing plants on the woodland floor a chance to thrive before the trees grow back. This cycle helps to keep the environment rich in species.

## Tree hugging

You can work out the approximate age of a tree by measuring its circumference 1.5m above the ground. In woodland, every 1cm equates to approximately one year. For a free-standing tree in open land, every 2cm represents one year.

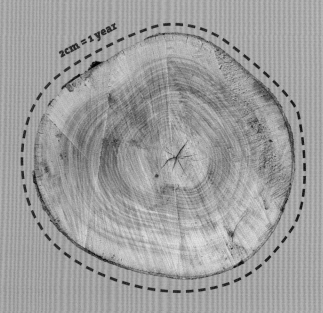

2cm = 1 year

# URBAN SPACES AND GARDENS

With ever-increasing urban sprawl, many animals and plants have had to learn to live side-by-side with humans. They've adapted to the constant noise and light produced by our way of life, and exploit the many food sources and opportunities that we provide.

## Plants

Certain plant species can be indicative of recently disturbed ground, and are a frequent sight on footpaths, towpaths and building sites. Stinging nettles, thistles, dandelions, brambles and buddleia are some of the most common you may find. In parks and gardens you're likely to come across sycamore and horse chestnut trees, along with fruit trees, roses and many flowering bulbs such as tulips, daffodils and crocuses.

## Mammals

A surprising number of mammals can be found in urban environments – foxes, squirrels, hedgehogs and in some places even deer. Some of the most commonly encountered animals are rats and mice – look out for them next time you're on the Underground or Metro…

# COMMON REPTILES

Although dinosaurs no longer roam the Lake District and alligators are rarely seen outside the zoo, our fields and forests are still home to a wide range of reptiles.

## Adder

It's often thought there are no venomous snakes in the UK. This is, in fact, rather wishful thinking. The adder is a member of the viper family, and although not usually fatal has a painful, poisonous bite. It's found throughout the UK, except, famously, in Ireland (where they were supposedly driven out by St Patrick).

It can be recognised by the zigzag markings on its back, spots on its side and a 'V' or 'X' on its head. Males are whitish/grey in colour while females are browner. They feed on mice and lizards and give birth to live young (not eggs) in late summer.

## Grass snake

As you'd expect from its name, the grass snake is usually green or brown. It's most frequently found near water, where it feeds on amphibians, notably live frogs and toads. Grass snakes are equally happy in woodland or in water, and are good swimmers. While they're non-venomous they'll still hiss and strike, while other defences include releasing an unpleasant garlic-scented odour and pretending to be dead!

## Slow-worm

It looks like a snake, it acts like a snake, but in fact the slow-worm is a lizard. Famous for its ability to shed its tail when being attacked, it's found in grassland and gardens throughout the UK. Although widespread, it isn't always easy to spot as it prefers dark, secluded spaces in compost heaps and under logs. It feeds on prey such as slugs and gives birth in late summer.

## Common lizard

Sometimes known as the viviparous lizard, the common lizard can be found creeping across the grasses and dry stone walls that criss-cross the UK. Around 15cm long, they have smooth rather than scaly skin (that's probably a newt) and are mostly brown, with stripes or spots. As sun lovers they alternate between exposed and covered areas, dining mainly on insects and spiders.

# COMMON UK BUTTERFLIES

The nation's butterflies are among our most attractive sights, showing off their colours and distinctive markings across our fields and gardens. Butterflies are one of the most glorious reminders of the abundance and variety of the natural world.

### Essex Skipper
Believe it or not, the Essex Skipper is most at home on motorway verges – and not just the M11 or M25, as it can now be found across the UK. Easily mistaken for the Small Skipper, the male can be distinguished from the female by the extra markings on its wings. It travels along the motorway corridors to all parts of the country.

### Holly Blue
Often seen in gardens around the UK, this pretty butterfly has suffered in numbers in recent years following particularly unpleasant attacks from the wasp Listrodomus nycthemerus. This aggressor lays eggs in the Holly Blue larvae, which is then used as food for the developing wasp.

### Red Admiral
The pop star of butterflies, the Red Admiral is seen and recognised in gardens across the country. Whereas it was once considered a visitor to the UK, it's now regarded as a year-round resident, though numbers can still fluctuate depending on food and climate.

### Duke of Burgundy
Despite its name, this butterfly is orange and brown in colour. The species is from the 'metalmarks' family, so named from the metallic appearance of some members. Females have six functional legs compared with the male's four, presumably to assist with multi-tasking! It's found mainly in central and southern England.

### Small Tortoiseshell
Although in decline, the Small Tortoiseshell is still a common sight in UK gardens. Adults can be seen in spring but become more common in summer while they collect nectar. Unfortunately the larvae can fall prey to a parasite, a fly called the Sturmia bella, whose eggs are consumed on the leaf. They hatch inside the larvae with predictably grisly consequences.

### Swallowtail
A member of the Papilionidae family, the Swallowtail is a large butterfly, related to the largest in the world – the birdwings. With their spectacular markings, rarity and unusual size, they are a coveted find. The wingspan of the male is generally between 75 and 82mm while the females can reach 85 to 92mm.

## Birds

House sparrows used to be a common sight in many towns and cities but since 1979 their numbers have dropped by 55%. Pigeons, starlings and gulls make the most of the various food sources available in towns and cities, and can often be seen in large flocks. Other common garden species include robins, blackbirds and blue tits.

## Invertebrates

Gardens are havens for all sorts of insects and mini-beasts. Look out for bees, wasps, beetles, ants, butterflies, spiders, slugs, snails, worms and more species of flies than you could ever imagine existed – there are as many as 7,000 varieties in the UK alone, with new ones still being found every year.

## Save the bees!

Einstein issued a dire warning about declining bee populations: 'If the bee disappears from the surface of the earth, man would have no more than four years to live. No more bees, no more pollination ... no more men!'

Whether this is strictly true or not is uncertain, but who are we to argue with Einstein? It's certainly the case that bees have a vital role in the pollination of crops, fruit and other plants. Here are some simple steps you can take to help them:

1  Avoid using pesticides.
2  Think about becoming a beekeeper.
3  Speak to your local authority and MP about what action they're taking.
4  Plant flowers and other bee-friendly flora in your garden.
5  Buy local honey.

## Protecting urban wildlife

Sadly many species and their habitats are harmed by humans, although mostly unintentionally. However, there are a surprising number of things you can do to help safeguard the future of our wildlife:

**1 Plant native plants in your garden**
Planting indigenous plants will provide food to the local animal, bird and insect population.

**2 Put out food**
A saucer of water for hedgehogs and nuts for birds will help them survive hard winters when food is much more scarce. But think carefully about cats and other predators, to ensure that you're not putting wildlife at risk.

**3 Drive slowly**
Our roads are full of road kill. A little more consideration when driving, especially in the countryside, will reduce the number of accidents that cause death and injury to our wildlife.

**4 Help prevent bird collisions**
Many birds die as a result of colliding with your windows – this can be avoided by putting up stickers or decals of birds, or drawing the curtains on very bright days.

**5 Avoid chemical herbicides and pesticides**
Yes, weeds are the bane of gardeners' lives, but consider the consequences of using harmful chemicals. Your garden is a delicate ecosystem, which can easily become imbalanced – harmful chemicals are slow to degrade, can poison soil, and are particularly harmful to frogs, toads and newts.

# LOWLAND HEATH

Heath is typically low, woody, shrubland that is now endangered in many parts of the UK. Whereas it once covered an area the size of Cornwall, it now spans an area barely larger than the Isle of Wight.

## Plants

Vegetation such as gorse and heather grow on the poor quality, acidic soil.

## Mammals

Although the heath is a permanent home to very few mammals, rabbits can often be seen, and it's a popular grazing ground for sheep and ponies.

## Heath or moor?

Some of our most mysterious wild places can be categorised as heath or moorland. They're largely uninhabited areas and reminders of our country when it was an emptier, more desolate place – the heath features in Shakespeare's King Lear, for example, as the setting for the king's wanderings in the storm.

Most people mistakenly consider the terms heath and moor to be interchangeable, but in fact they're distinct habitats.

Like heath, moorland is largely uninhabited and uncultivated by people but again boasts a surprisingly large amount of flora and fauna. Moorlands are also popular as dramatic stages in literature – just think of *Wuthering Heights* or *The Hound of the Baskervilles* – probably because of their ghostly associations.

## Birds

Heath is an important habitat for birds that breed and feed there, such as nightjars, stone curlews and Dartford warblers.

## Invertebrates

The ladybird spider, silver-studded blue butterfly, heather beetle, sand wasp, heath bee-fly, heath tiger beetle and raft spider are examples of smaller creatures that live on heaths. They are found at the bottom of the food chain, but many larger creatures depend on them for survival.

## Kestrel

A member of the falcon family, the kestrel has a long tail and pointed wings and can often be seen hovering over fields looking for rodents and smaller birds. They can be found anywhere, from heath and moorland to towns and cities, perched on a high vantage point on the lookout for food.

# THREATS TO HEATHLAND HABITATS

UK lowland heaths face many threats and consequently are recognised as a priority habitat under the UK Biodiversity Action Plan (UK BAP). Sensitive management of the habitat is needed to protect it against these specific dangers:

- Inappropriate management – to ensure heath remains in a favourable condition it needs regular grazing, controlled burning and preventative action to stop the encroachment of bracken, scrub and trees. In past years, many sites have not got this delicate balance right.

- Loss of habitat – conversion to farmland together with the spread of urban development has destroyed much heathland and left other areas dangerously fragmented.

- Leisure and tourism – trampling and erosion threaten the very habitat that people have come to visit. This is not to mention the damage and disturbance from noise, litter and dog fouling.

- Pollution – nutrients can be deposited onto lowland heath via the air, changing the acidity and nutrient levels of the soil. Wet heaths are also very susceptible to pollutants in the water supply.

- Disease – any disease affecting the plant species on the heathland can have an obvious negative effect on the habitat.

# UK NATIONAL PARKS

## Cairngorms

Protecting Scotland's highest mountain range, this park covering 1,367 square miles of the East Highlands also boasts spectacular rivers, lochs, farmland and wilderness.

## Lake District

Inspiring generations of poets, painters, walkers and climbers, the Lake District cover 900 square miles. Its longest lake is Windermere at 10.5 miles, and its deepest is Wastwater at 79m.

## Snowdonia

Spanning 823 square miles, Snowdonia offers breathtaking mountains and jaw-dropping views, receiving over 10 million visitors each year. Half a million people reach the summit of Snowdonia itself (1,085m) annually.

## Exmoor

Covering large parts of Devon and Somerset, Exmoor spans 267 square miles. Its coast has the highest and lowest tides in Europe and the highest sea cliffs on the British mainland. The Exmoor pony is now rarer than the giant panda.

## Loch Lomond

Covering an area of 720 square miles, this National Park – called Loch Lomond and the Trossachs – has 21 Munros, 19 Corbetts, 22 large lochs and 50 rivers! See page 21 for more information about Munros and Corbetts.

## Dartmoor

This is an area of rugged moorland covering 368 square miles in the heart of Devon. Roughly the same size as Greater London, its highest point is High Willhays at 621m.

## Peak District

One of the most popular areas for walking, cycling and climbing in England, the Peak District has 1,600 miles of footpaths and 58 miles of cycle trails; the highest point is Kinder Scout (636m).

## National Parks

Established to protect beautiful and unspoilt areas of our countryside, there are now 15 National Parks across the UK.

**Brecon Beacons**
**Broads**
**Cairngorms**
**Dartmoor**
**Exmoor**
**Lake District**
**Loch Lomond**
**New Forest**
**Northumberland**
**North York Moors**
**Peak District**
**Pembrokeshire Coast**
**Snowdonia**
**South Downs**
**Yorkshire Dales**

## New Forest

Home to the largest remaining area of lowland heath in Europe, the New Forest is a haven for wildlife across its 150 square miles. Surprisingly, only half of the park is woodland.

# UPLAND HEATH
# AND MOOR

Whereas heath is largely low-lying, moorland is chiefly found in upland areas. You just need to think of place names such as Dartmoor, Exmoor, Bodmin Moor and the Yorkshire Moors to know how extensive these are in the British Isles.

## Vegetation

Mosses, heather, bracken and grass are the staple fare on Britain's moors, and usually grow on peat-rich earth.

## Mammals

Only the hardiest animals are able to survive on the exposed moors; these include the Exmoor pony and Scottish blackface sheep.

## Birds

Curlew, skylark, golden plover, harrier and merlin are just some of the birds that swoop across the open skies above our moorlands. Their calls across the empty landscape are evocative of such remote and wild places.

# LOW-LYING WETLANDS

Swamp, bog, marsh, fen, peat land – all are different types of wetland that can be found across the UK. Not only are wetlands a good sink for atmospheric carbon but they are also some of the best natural flood defences available.

## Vegetation

Wetland soil has very low oxygen levels, and so the vegetation has adapted to thrive in otherwise hostile conditions. Bogs, (such as those found on the Humberhead Levels) are often characterised by sphagnum moss, whereas the fens and reedbeds common in Norfolk and parts of Cambridgeshire are recognisable from the sedges, rushes and reeds found there.

## Mammals

Water voles and otters can be found on wetlands, along with water shrews and hares. Sometimes you may even see Chinese Water Deer, a species identified by large, protruding tusks often used as weapons.

## Shaping the land

Across the UK, many wetlands have suffered extensive damage through drainage, pollution and development. A lot of work is now being done to restore these wetlands to their original condition as a means of reducing flooding and water pollution. Controlling the water levels, altering the river channels and planting native species of vegetation are all methods people are utilising to try and reinstate the natural functions of these landscapes.

## Birds

Wetlands are often havens for migrating birds as they are a very important source of food. Waders, warblers, ducks and geese are common sights either in or alongside the water.

## Insects

Low-lying wetlands are an ideal habitat for insects, which live submerged below the water, float on the surface or hover just above it. There are an amazing 50,000 insects and invertebrates that make wetlands their home.

# WADING BIRDS

As the name suggests, these are birds that frequent shallow waters, marshes, flooded meadows and the edges of ponds and lakes. This is also where they find their food – a diet of fish, insects and amphibians.

## Snipe

Snipe are widespread across the UK, but less common in the south-west. The snipe is classed as an amber species due to its slight decline in numbers over the past 25 years. Males produce a distinctive, thin tweeting noise, known as 'drumming' when displaying. This noise is produced by the wind whistling through its spread outer tail feathers.

## Lapwing

A familiar farmland bird of low-lying areas, also found on wetlands, the lapwing is also known as the peewit, due to the sound of its display calls. Lapwings eat worms and other insects, and can sometimes be seen feeding at night, especially if there is a bright moon.

## Curlew

The curlew is Europe's largest wading bird, and has seen a clear change in its distribution across the UK due to changes in land use. Its down-curved bill allows it to dig through estuarine mud for shellfish, worms and shrimps.

## Oystercatcher

With its strong bill, the oystercatcher's diet consists mainly of cockles and mussels. Found along most coasts of the UK, the greatest populations can be found at major estuaries, such as Morecambe Bay, where cockle farming is common. The oystercatcher is the national bird of the Faroe Islands.

## Bittern

The bittern is one of the most threatened bird species in the UK due to its dependence on a very specific type of habitat – reed beds. A lot of work has been done to try and increase the UK population, although they can still only be found mainly in East Anglia and Lancashire. Bitterns are also famous for their booming call which can carry for over a kilometre.

## Heron

Grey herons are a fairly common sight across the whole of the UK, by almost any source of water (including garden ponds!). These large birds can be up to a metre in length and have a wing span of nearly two metres. Although their diet mainly consists of small fish, they have been known to take small mammals, amphibians and even small birds such as ducklings.

# SEA AND COASTLINE

As an island nation, we're never far from the sea. From Dorset's Jurassic coast to the wild, empty beaches of Northumberland, we're bordered by thousands of miles of dramatic coastline, most of which is free for all of us to enjoy.

## Vegetation

On salty, windy coasts a unique variety of flora has evolved over time to include such exotic fare as Lunday cabbage, oyster plants near the Giant's Causeway, and spider orchids at Purbeck.

## Mammals

From Welsh mountain ponies to grey seals in Norfolk and elsewhere, our coasts boast a thriving ecology, including dolphins, porpoises and whales that swim within sight of our shores.

## The UK's coastline

As well as representing some of the best walking environments, our coast is home to a superabundance of wildlife, on the land, in the air and in the sea.

Think of the coast and you'll picture sandy beaches, yet these represent less than 30% of our coastline. Saltmarsh, grass, shingle, rocks and mud are the predominant terrains on our beaches. It's therefore hard to generalise about flora and fauna, which gives coastal areas their attractive variety.

## Birds

The UK is a stopping-off point for millions of migrating birds, giving us a free display of the world's wildlife right on our doorstep. From the grey plover on their journey towards Siberia to the black-tailed godwit heading towards Iceland, the UK is a global crossroads. Perhaps most dramatic is the sight of the hundreds of thousands of geese which descend on the UK each winter.

## Crustaceans

Crustaceans are animals without a backbone; their distinguishing features are normally five pairs of legs and two pairs of antennae and a cephalothorax – the protective crust which gives them their name. They live either in the sea or on the seashore, breathing with gills, like fish. They vary in size from tiny copepods, which float on the surface of the sea, to large crabs and lobsters.

## Leatherback turtle

The leatherback turtle is a common species found on UK shores, measuring up to 2m and weighing up to 600kg. As our native waters grow increasingly warmer they're becoming a more common sight, and can be identified by their size and distinctive leather-like shells. Their diet consists mainly of jellyfish.

These outdoor aquariums are often small ecosystems in their own right.

### Topshells

Easily spotted by their pointed, spiral shells, topshells are found in shallow water and rocky shores. They feed on algae.

### Periwinkles

These marine snails are found on rocks and in and around coastal mud flats. They form part of the diet of many coastal birds.

### Cockles

More familiar as a tasty snack, these 'bivalve' marine molluscs live buried in the sand just below the low-tide mark.

### Barnacles

A kind of arthropod and a member of the crustacean family, the barnacle lives in a fixed place – for example on the hull of a ship.

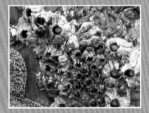

### Razor shell

Found on sandy beaches inside a thin, open-ended shell, razor shells (or fish) burrow down into the sand using a single strong foot.

### Mermaid's Purse

This is actually the egg capsule of a shark or skate. The size varies, but they measure around 10cm and are normally found empty.

# RIVERS AND RIVERBANKS

The British Isles are irrigated by a network of interconnected rivers, the names of which define our geography. It's impossible to think of the north-east of England without the names of the Tyne and Tees, or the west without the names of the Mersey, the Wye and the Severn.

## Vegetation

As well as playing a vital role in providing water for agriculture and draining water from the fields, riverbanks play host to a huge variety of plant life. In addition to providing a home for many water-loving flowers, such as flag iris and marsh marigold, they're also the habitat of three specialised plant categories: mosses, submerged plants and algae.

Mosses attach themselves to rocks in or near the water, while algae are free-floating without leaves or shoots – examples include plankton algae and stonewort. Submerged plants are attached to the riverbed and include waterweed, pondweeds and even wild celery.

## Mammals

Otters and voles (often mistakenly called 'water rats') can be seen on many UK rivers – though you'll need to be quiet and patient. Foreign interlopers such as mink and coypu are also becoming widespread.

## Birds

The heron, kingfisher and crested grebe are just some of the beautiful birds to look out for on the river, alongside egrets, swans, cormorants, coots and many different types of geese and ducks.

# COMMON BRITISH FISH

Our rivers are teeming with fish of every size and description; here are some of the most common fish found in the UK. Of course, there are many others – so let this just be the start of your journey of discovery.

## Trout

While trout are mainly freshwater fish, some varieties will divide their time between estuaries and the sea, generally returning to rivers to spawn. Their markings vary depending on their environment – if returning from the sea, they're silver in colour; if in rivers, they can be marked and highly coloured. While they feed on small insects, larger trout will consume other fish up to a third of their own length.

## Carp

Described as the 'queen of rivers', the carp is a coarse fish that can live up to 30 years and grow to inordinate size. Although they're generally up to 30cm in length, the very largest can reach over 1m in length and weigh up to a staggering 40kg. Most have a high-ridged back and all carp are notoriously difficult to fish.

## Pike

Pike (or northern pike) are generally olive green in colour with reddish fins. They grow to as much as 1.5m in length can weigh over 20kg. Their diet consists of other fish (including pike), as well as voles and ducklings. They're able to 'tread' water, remaining still before suddenly attacking their prey and taking them unawares in their sharp teeth.

## Perch

The perch is generally rounder and longer than the other freshwater fish mentioned here, with two dorsal fins – the first spiny and the second soft. They feed mainly on insect larvae and other fish, and lay their eggs in strings near the protection of underwater plants. Perch weigh between 0.5kg and 2kg.

## Roach

One of the smaller fish, the roach typically measures between 35mm and 45mm and is most easily identified by its red fins and silver blue colour. It also has a distinctive eye – a red spot near the pupil. Some older fish will be larger than the younger or middle-aged specimens.

## Eel

Scientists have recently discovered that eels lead amazing and long lives. When mature, they leave European coasts to swim across the Atlantic and spawn in the warm waters of the Sargasso Sea, near Bermuda. The young then return over the course of three years or more, initially as transparent 'elvers' living in the darkness and mud of river beds and under rocks.

# PREDICTING THE WEATHER

You can't choose your weather, but you can certainly prepare for it, and even use it to your advantage. From harnessing the sun's rays to lighting a fire to collecting rainwater to drink, the weather should be thought of as friend rather than foe.

## Wind

Wind is caused by the interaction of warm and cold air. As air warmed by the sun rises, it pulls cooler air below it; and when it gradually cools it sinks again and in turn displaces the warmed air that had replaced it. This air movement creates wind, and shifting wind causes changes in the weather.

Weather is measured using the Beaufort scale, which was devised by Admiral Francis Beaufort in 1805. It's widely used around the world as a way of measuring the force of the wind based on the visible effect it has on land and sea. Changes in the wind signify a change in the weather, and the greater the force of the wind the more severe the change will be.

## Beaufort wind force scale

| | Specifications and equivalent speeds | | | | | | | | |
|---|---|---|---|---|---|---|---|---|---|
| Beaufort wind scale | Mean wind speed | | Limits of wind speed | | Wind descriptive terms | Probable wave height in metres* | Probable maximum wave height in metres* | Seastate | Sea descriptive terms |
| | Knots | ms$^{-1}$ | Knots | ms$^{-1}$ | | | | | |
| 0 | 0 | 0 | <1 | <1 | Calm | - | - | 0 | Calm (glassy) |
| 1 | 2 | 1 | 1–3 | 1–2 | Light air | 0.1 | 0.1 | 1 | Calm (rippled) |
| 2 | 5 | 3 | 4–6 | 2–3 | Light breeze | 0.2 | 0.3 | 2 | Smooth (wavelets) |
| 3 | 9 | 5 | 7–10 | 4–5 | Gentle breeze | 0.6 | 1.0 | 3 | Slight |
| 4 | 13 | 7 | 11–16 | 6–8 | Moderate breeze | 1.0 | 1.5 | 3–4 | Slight–Moderate |
| 5 | 19 | 10 | 17–21 | 9–11 | Fresh breeze | 2.0 | 2.5 | 4 | Moderate |
| 6 | 24 | 12 | 22–27 | 11–14 | Strong breeze | 3.0 | 4.0 | 5 | Rough |
| 7 | 30 | 15 | 28–33 | 14–17 | Near gale | 4.0 | 5.5 | 5–6 | Rough–Very rough |
| 8 | 37 | 19 | 34–40 | 17–21 | Gale | 5.5 | 7.5 | 6–7 | Very rough–High |
| 9 | 44 | 23 | 41–47 | 21–24 | Severe gale | 7.0 | 10.0 | 7 | High |
| 10 | 52 | 27 | 48–55 | 25–28 | Storm | 9.0 | 12.5 | 8 | Very High |
| 11 | 60 | 31 | 56–63 | 29–32 | Violent storm | 11.5 | 16.0 | 8 | Very High |
| 12 | - | - | 64+ | 33+ | Hurricane | 14+ | - | 9 | Phenomenal |

\* 1  These values refer to well-developed wind waves of the open sea.

2  The lag effect between the wind getting up and the sea increasing should be borne in mind.

3  To convert knots to miles per hour multiply by 1.15; for metres per second multiply by 0.514.

# WEATHER LORE

For centuries shepherds, farmers and sailors have looked to the skies for indications of the weather to come. Without the benefit of radio shipping forecasts or updates on iPads they relied on received wisdom to help them plan for the hours and days ahead. Here are some of the most popular and therefore possibly more reliable proverbs; be warned, however, that since climate differs from country to country they cannot be relied on absolutely.

'Rain before seven,
fine before eleven'

'Rain long foretold, long last;
Short notice, soon will pass'

'Three days' rain will
empty any sky'

'Dew on the grass, rain
won't come to pass'

'Flies will swarm
before a storm'

'Sound travelling far and
wide, a stormy day betide'

'Cold is the night when
the stars shine bright'

'Ash leaf before the oak, then
we will have a summer soak.
Oak leaf before the ash, the summer
comes without a splash'

'Red sky at night, shepherds'
delight. Red sky in the morning,
shepherds' warning'

## Weather indicators

Believe it or not, you can get a fair indication of the weather just by taking a deep breath. If the air is very pungent, either with sweet-smelling flowers or with compost-like odours as plants release their waste, then wet weather is on the way. When the air contains more moisture, scents are stronger.

Most people know that cows lie down before a thunderstorm. They also tend to huddle together before bad weather. You'll also notice fewer seagulls in the sky at the coast if a storm's on the way. Almost all animals become subdued before rain. Rows of birds on telegraph wires usually indicate low pressure, and therefore fair weather.

If you see dew on the grass in the morning it's an indicator of fair weather – there's little breeze to bring rainclouds your way. If it's dry, this means that the air has been dried by a breeze, which can often bring inclement weather. Forget all of the above if it rained during the night!

Why not use this schoolboy's favourite to predict the weather: if there's moisture in the air, the scales on a pine cone will close, which means that rain's on the way; but if it's going to be fine the scales will dry up and open.

# CLOUD SPOTTING

Cloud spotting has become recognised as an art in its own right; it's easier than you think and allows you to predict weather conditions with surprising accuracy.

### Stratus
These stretch over a wide area and can often cover the sky for as far as the eye can see. Stratus are low-lying clouds (fog is actually stratus cloud) and don't often result in much rain.

### Cirrus
These fine, feather-like clouds aren't likely to produce rain either. They can indicate a change in weather conditions.

### Nimbus
You don't need to be a weatherman to know that these clouds spell rain. They're the classic gathering storm clouds.

### Cumulus
When you see a cloud in a child's picture book, it's more than likely to be a cumulus – they're the classic fluffy cloud and indicate fair weather if white, or rain if dark.

### Altocumulus
Patchy cloud, at medium height; low chance of rain.

### Cumulonimbus
An oversized cumulus cloud, which can indicate storms, rain and hail.

## Northern Lights (aurora borealis)

These spectacular light displays can be seen in the northernmost parts of the Northern Hemisphere. Usually a fluorescent green glow with a hint of red, they are caused by charged particles from the sun colliding with molecules in the Earth's atmosphere. Although more spectacular in the polar regions, the Northern Lights can sometimes be seen in Scotland just before or after midnight.

### Altostratus
This cloud acts like a screen over the sun and usually indicates a deterioration in the weather.

### Nimbostratus
Sheets of dark grey cloud, which indicate heavy rain.

### Noctilucent
High, thin blue/white clouds seen in the summer just after sunset. Made up of water crystals high up in the Earth's atmosphere, they can be naturally occurring or created by water droplets from spacecraft.

### Stratocumulus
Low, lumpy cloud that indicates light rain.

### Cirrocumulus
This is what's sometimes referred to as 'mackerel sky' and is most often seen on cold winter days. Little chance of rain.

### Cirrostratus
Thin sheets of clouds that can spell light rain or drizzle. Can cover the whole sky and act as a screen, for example causing 'hazy sunshine', or cause a halo effect around the sun or moon.

# TENTS AND CAMPING

The legendary camper Showell Styles once described tents as 'houses on poles'. However, he also made the point that the camper doesn't live in a tent (which really should be used only for sleeping) but in the open air. Whether on your own or in a large group, there's a real sense of liberation and freedom to be had from a truly great camping trip. But there are three sure-fire ways to spoil it: poor equipment, poor knowledge and poor organisation. Spending hours trying to put up a cheap, low-quality tent in the dark, without knowing what you're doing, is enough to put you off camping forever.

# CHOOSING A TENT

The first and most important item of your kit is the tent. If you're camping in a large group (for example at a Scout camp) then a Patrol Tent is the sensible option. If on a hiking trip, then a lightweight tent is obviously more suitable.

### Ridge or A-frame

The traditional A-Frame is now making something of a comeback as a design classic. Essentially it works on the same principle as it always has – a pole at each end of a single rectangular space with sloping sides. To maintain its shape it needs to be pegged securely on all sides. While scoring maximum points for retro chic, however, it does have the disadvantage of sagging walls – which must be avoided unless you want to get yourself or your kit wet.

### Dome tent

Probably the best-selling variety, the dome tent is the mainstay of campsites and festivals the world over. With a square or rectangular floor space it is pitched by inserting and securing two glass-fibre or aluminium alloy poles that cross over at the top. Once taut, the inner tent can be hung, or outer attached as appropriate, and then the whole thing pegged down.

### Hoop or tunnel tent

More spacious than the dome tent, these have a longer body shape and therefore are not freestanding in the same way as the dome. They rely on tension from pegged guy lines to maintain their shape. These are the tents of choice for family camping as they can have a number of separate compartments (or 'rooms'). Pitching is normally by inserting two hoops into sleeves which are held in pockets at each end. Again, the inner tent(s) may be hung inside the outer tent.

## Bivy/solo tent

Recent advances in tent technology have meant that ultra-compact, lightweight tents are now available. A good bivy/solo tent weighs around a kilogram but provides perfect protection from the elements. With approximate dimensions of 65cm high and 230cm long, there's just enough room to change out of wet clothes before bedding down for the night.

Also available is the bivy bag. Weighing little more than half a kilogram, this is a weatherproof sack that completely covers you and your sleeping bag. It should be used only in extreme conditions, for example if your main tent has become torn or otherwise damaged.

*Small but perfectly formed: the bivy/solo tent is a miracle of modern camping technology.*

## Tarp and hammock

Using a hammock beneath a tarp is the preferred combination for every true outdoorsman/woman. Suspended between two trees by a pair of shoelace knots and protected from light showers by a weatherproof tarpaulin, you can drift off to sleep listening to the wind in the leaves and the scurrying of creatures of the forest.

# TENT CARE

When camping in the cold and wet, your tent is all that keeps you from the elements. The least you can do is to give it some proper care and attention.

### Tent care checklist

- Tents should be regularly checked, cleaned and repaired if necessary to ensure they remain in prime condition. The best time is before you camp. There's little worse than turning up at camp to discover a missing pole or a broken zip.

- Check for broken pegging points. Sometimes elastic can be frayed, so pull to check. Likewise, glass-fibre poles with hairline splits will shatter when bent into position. Undo knotted guy lines and tie them correctly. Check you have the correct number and type of pegs required and replace zips if faulty.

- If your tent is still wet when you break camp (ie pack up) then unpack it again as soon as you arrive home. Allow it to air on the washing line, shed or garage until it is fully dry. A wet tent left in its bag will soon attract mildew. Sometimes it helps to detach the guy lines as these take longer to dry and can be left separate.

- If your tent has been attacked by mildew, try scrubbing gently. If this fails to remove it, you may need to use a specialist formula such as MiraZyme, which should work.

- To clean your tent, scrub gently and use a non-detergent soap and water. Avoid commercial products such as washing-up liquid as this can damage the layer of waterproof protection that was applied to your tent at manufacture. Whatever you do, avoid putting your tent in the washing machine – it could tear or even melt!

- Try and avoid too much direct sunlight on your tent (easy when camping in the UK!) as the ultraviolet rays can degrade the fibres. Camp where you know there will be some shade.

- Most minor rips in your tent can be repaired by applying nylon repair tape, leaving plenty of tape on all sides of the tear. Smooth the tape entirely flat to create a seal, then treat with a commercial seam sealer.

# LIGHTWEIGHT TENTS

There are several types of hike, or lightweight, tents. The two most popular are dome tents and A-frame tents. Illustrated below are the general methods of pitching these. You need to check the manufacturer's instructions and practise erecting the tents before going to camp.

Ventilation flap

Entry flap

Curved ridge poll

Guy lines

Groundsheet

Mosquito flap

Flysheet

Loops

*A dome tent - one of the easiest lightweight tents to pitch.*

## Pop-up tents

Tents are available that 'pop' open when released, and some have inflatable rather than steel poles (more convenient, but more expensive). Pop-ups are becoming more popular, especially on the festival scene. They are useful for overnight stays and the double-lined ones are fine for long weekends although not much more unless good weather is guaranteed. Larger sized pop-ups are now available for four people but require two people to pitch. Although easy to use and cheap, pop-up tents score quite poorly in terms of quality and durability.

## Getting started

Once you have removed the tent from its bag, check that you have all the necessary components before you begin putinmg up the tent. Most lightweight tents can be erected by a single person.

Let's take a dome tent as an example. The task would be started by pegging the back edge of the tent in the corners and sliding the poles in towards the locating rings at the points that have been pegged. Once in these locating rings, the poles can be assembled and bent over like a pair of diagonal arches, then secured in the locating rings on the opposite side to form the dome.

With the main dome up, continue to peg down and extend the guy lines for stability, especially in windy conditions. A tunnel tent would follow a similar procedure but with a series of arches and no diagonal poles.

# PITCHING A LIGHTWEIGHT TENT

**1** Find a suitable piece of flat ground. Empty the tent from its bag or case and lay out all the components on the ground.

**2** Assemble the poles, which are usually connected with elastic, and insert them through the sleeves in the outer tent. Ensure that the ends are clipped into the eyelets or rings attached to the bottom edge of the outer tent.

**3** Insert the pegs through the rubber loops and stretch out the outer tent so that all sides are taut.

**4** If the inner tent isn't already attached to the outer, open the door and, using the toggles, attach the inner. Peg out the inner tent and any guy lines on the outer.

## Variations

There are several variations of lightweight tent. For example, with some tents the inner is erected first and the outer laid over the top. With others the outer is erected first and then the inner is clipped onto the poles on the inside. Some tents are a combination of the above to enable ease of pitching.

# PATROL RIDGE TENT

The traditional Patrol tent consists of two or three upright poles, green canvas, plus a flysheet in many cases, four main storm guys and a number of side guys. It requires a minimum of three people to pitch it, and it's strongly recommend that everyone who'll be helping to erect it takes the time to familiarise themselves with the parts beforehand and practise pitching it at home.

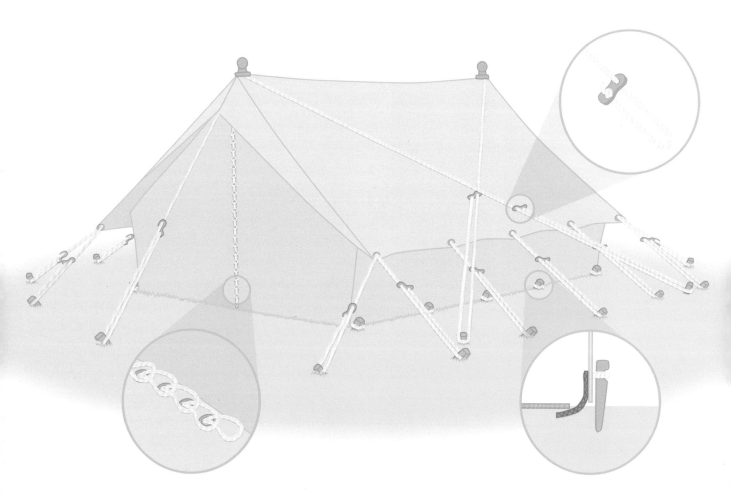

## Getting started

Find a flat piece of ground free of sharp objects and facing away from prevailing wind. Empty the tent from its bag or case and lay out all the components on the ground. Lay out the groundsheet in the intended position of the tent. Put a peg in the ground at each of the four corners. Open out the flysheet and tent on the ground.

While the tent is on the ground, carry out a visual inspection to ensure nothing has been damaged while in transit or during unpacking. Now is a good time to explain the stages in advance to those helping pitch the tent and to indicate who will be doing what. This will be home for the days and nights to come, so it's worth taking your time and doing it correctly.

# PITCHING A PATROL TENT

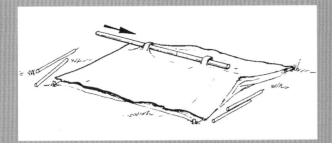

**1** Assemble the ridge and upright poles and feed the ridgepole through all the loops attached to the ridge of the tent. Take care not to stand on the canvas whilst you do this and be careful not to damage the canvas with the ridge pole. One way to ensure this is to lie on the canvas and feed the ridge through gently.

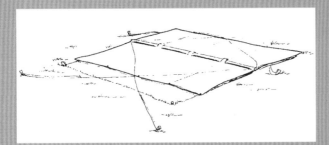

**2** Sort out the tent pegs into their different sizes. Put in four large pegs for the main guy lines. Don't put the pegs in too deeply at this stage, as they'll probably have to be moved later.

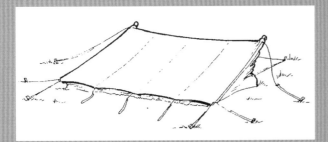

**3** Place the spikes on the upright poles through the holes in the ridge pole and corresponding eyelets. Once this is done the tent can be folded over along the ridge. Attach the main guy lines to the previously placed pegs. Put the dollies, attached to the storm guys, over the spikes of the upright poles.

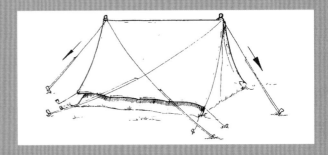

**4** Stand the tent upright, raising both of the uprights together to avoid bending the spikes. Two people are needed, one to hold each of the uprights until the main guy lines have been tightened. The tent should now be upright but rather unsteady. Lace or tie up the doors of the tent, then peg out the door and corner brailings.

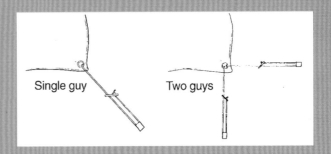

Single guy       Two guys

**5** Peg out the other guy lines, corner ones first, using large tent pegs. Generally, if a corner has one guy rope it's pitched at 45°, or if it has two they're pitched at 90°. A peg should be placed so that when the guy line is taut, the runner is about one-third of the way up from the peg. The side guy line pegs should be parallel with the ridge pole and the guy lines following the tent seams.

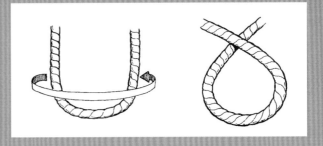

**6** Using smaller pegs, loop and peg out all the brailings to keep the tent walls vertical. The brailings should be looped before being attached to the peg as this helps to prevent them from slipping off.

# OVERHEAD COVER

The tarp and hammock is a Scouting classic and can be used in the right weather as a refreshing change to the more common tent and roll mat combination. Suspended above the forest floor and protected from light showers, it's the perfect way to sleep in the open.

## Tarp and hammock

The tarp shown on this page measures 3m square, weighs 650g and has 19 fixing points, which means it can be pitched in any number of ways – three configurations are shown in the photos on this page. You can even do away with trees and make a tent-like, open-fronted shelter with one or two sticks and a guy rope for support at the entrance.

It's normal to have four guy lines attached to a tarp, with two spares. Some guy lines have small elastic loops and mini karabiners between the lines and fixings to make them easy to replace in the event someone catches a line with their foot.

It's a good idea to mark the fixing points needed for the standard and diamond configurations so that you can get the ridge line in both quickly and correctly, which all helps when it's either raining or getting dark.

Poles can also be used at the corners to lift or lower the tarp, which gives plenty of flexibility depending on the weather conditions.

The hammock shown opposite measures 2.7m x 1.4m, weighs 700g and has a zipped compartment, which is ideal for a foam sleeping mat.

## Tips for setting up a wild camp

- Check there are no dead branches above you, and avoid beech trees, as they have a reputation for dropping branches with no warning!
- Find two robust trees about 3–4m apart (depending on the size of your tarp).
- Erect the tarp first; you can then finish off the hammock while being protected from any adverse weather.
- Secure the hammock at waist height, ensuring it's taut.

## Putting up the tarp

There are two main quick-release knots used to assemble the tarp. The first is the Evenk hitch (aka Siberian hitch), named after the reindeer herders who used it because it needed only one glove taken off to tie (see opposite). The second is the tarp tension knot, which is secure and adds tension to the ridge line.

## Putting up your hammock

To secure your hammock, use a simple shoelace knot but double knot the bunny ears. Insert either a forked branch or the standing end of the knot into the loops as added security.

## Knots used in the tarp system

- Tarp tension knot
- Evenk hitch
- Prussic knot
- Lark's head. Run a length of paracord tree-to-tree just under the tarp and use this to keep your storage bags safe
- Highwayman's hitch. To hang your boots and light up with for easy reach at night
- Doubled shoelace knot
- Sheepshank
- Adjustable loop

This is a fairly typical basic set-up. You can use different knots and systems but these will see you right until you find what works best for you. When you're woken by the morning sun to a quiet forest view, you'll know that the effort of setting up your wild camp was worth it.

# EVENK HITCH

Used to attach rope to a fixed object (in this case a tree), the Evenk hitch is a secure knot, easy to tie and quick to release.

**1** Take the cordage clockwise round the tree and wrap it around two fingers as shown.

**2** Hold the two lengths together in your right hand and point your left hand down.

**3** Then point your left hand up.

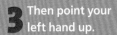

**4** Reach over and grab the non-looped working length of cordage and pull through the loop around your fingers.

**5** Pull until the knot is sound. Once you've positioned the knot height-wise, push the knot to the tree and place a forked stick or the standing end of the knot in the loop.

**6** To secure your hammock, use a shoelace knot, but double-knot the bunny ears. With all three of these insert either a forked branch or the standing end of the knot into the loops.

# SLEEPING BAGS AND MATS

Quality sleep is important. If you've been kept awake all night by the cold, you'll certainly suffer for it the next day. There's nothing worse than watching others sleeping soundly and then feeling bleary and tired yourself in the morning.

## Types of sleeping bag

Sleeping bags work by trapping warm air within the bag while you sleep. They use the heat generated by your body and circulate it without releasing it. The best kind of sleeping bags are those with features that help retain this heat, whether it's a top-of-the-range filling, baffles that keep draughts out, or a hood that stops warmth escaping from around your head.

## Filling

The type of filling in your sleeping bag has a huge bearing on its warmth. Cheaper products use synthetic fillings, the most popular synthetic material being Polyester. There are then different grades, from Hollowfibre (a collection of Polyester fibres) to Micraloft, which comprises much finer layers of Polyester, meaning that the bag does not take up as much space when it is packed away. An advantage of synthetic filling is that it doesn't generally lose its insulating qualities if wet.

Bags filled with down (from duck and geese) are an excellent choice for cold weather expeditions. They are light, warm and durable, but cost more. The downside (no pun intended) is that they lose insulating qualities if wet, and must be washed carefully. Duck down is cheaper that goose down, but is approximately 25% less efficient as an insulator.

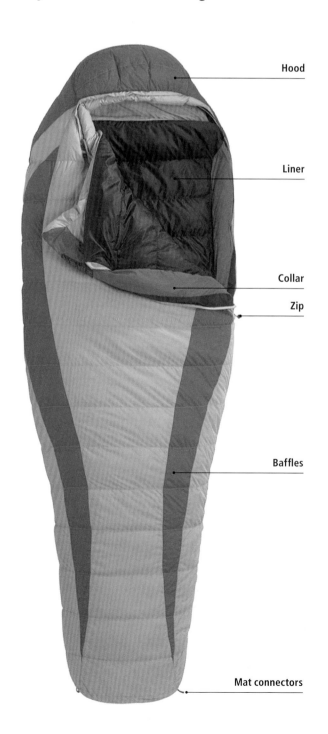

Hood

Liner

Collar

Zip

Baffles

Mat connectors

## The first sleeping bag

Legend has it that Robert Louis Stevenson, the author of *Treasure Island*, invented the first ever sleeping bag, during his adventures in France described in *Travels with a Donkey in the Cévennes*. He wanted a practical, self-contained and portable sleeping blanket. However, the fleece-lined sack produced was so heavy it could only be carried on his donkey!

## Sleeping bag ratings

Sleeping bags have ratings so that you get an idea of what would be comfortable in the summer and what would be better in winter.

When buying a sleeping bag, therefore, look carefully at its rating and the maximum and minimum temperatures at which it's claimed the bag will keep you warm. Here's a rough guide of how sleeping bags are rated:

**1 season**
Really only for use in the summer; usually around +4°/5°.

**2 season**
Good for late spring and early autumn, when it's not sweltering and you're unlikely to be on the receiving end of cold snaps or snow; around 0°.

**3 season**
Best for mild to cold nights, but with a very low temperature; 0° to –5°.

**4 season**
These are made for very cold winter nights in the outdoors and are typically more bulky and weigh more, but they do keep you exceptionally warm; –5° to –10°.

**5 season**
Specialist bags for expedition use; these are probably too warm for most activities in the UK.

## Sleeping mats

No matter how good your sleeping bag, if you're lying on cold wet ground, you won't sleep soundly. A standard foam sleeping mat effectively does two things. Firstly, it provides an insulating later between you and the ground. Secondly, it prevents ground damp from seeping into your sleeping bag. The thicker the foam, the better the insulation it will provide, but think about the extra space this will take up in your kit.

# KEEPING IT CLEAN

Camping can be a muddy business, so make sure you know how to wash your sleeping bag.

- Sleeping bag liners are usually made of cotton or silk. Cotton is cheaper but silk is lighter and takes up less room. Liners perform two important functions: they keep your sleeping bag clean, reducing the need to wash it, and they can add 1–2° to the bag's warmth rating because of the extra layer of material and air.

- On your return from camp, remove the sleeping bag from its sack and sponge away any obvious dirt.

- Check the label for any special washing instructions and also to determine the type of filling.

- Ensure the bag is fully zipped up before washing.

- The bag can either be washed by hand or in a washing machine.

- If it has down filling, use only a mild soap. Do not use detergent or fabric softener as these may damage your sleeping bag.

- Bags with synthetic fillings can be washed with detergent and softener.

- Run the wash again without soap to ensure the sleeping bag is rinsed thoroughly.

- Gently press the water out – don't wring its neck!

- To dry the bag, open it up fully on an indoor drying rack or pegged to an outdoor washing line.

- Use of a tumbledrier should be avoided as it wastes energy, but if you have no alternative then keep it on a very low heat setting and check regularly.

# PACKING YOUR RUCKSACK

Personal equipment may be packed in a holdall, rucksack or large bag. Avoid suitcases as they take up valuable storage space when empty. If you've packed for someone else then ensure they know what has been included and excluded.

## Guidelines for packing your rucksack

- Put the items you need easy access to at the top of the rucksack or in the side pockets.
- Disperse the weight so it's easy and comfortable to carry.
- Take care to ensure that easily damaged items are stowed carefully in the pockets.
- Pack clothes in a plastic bag (or bin liner) to keep them dry.
- A sleeping mat can be carried beneath the rucksack in a plastic bag, or secured to the top.
- Light, bulky items should be placed near the bottom and heavier items at the top – this will make the rucksack easier to carry, especially over longer distances

*Pack your rucksack in a logical manner, with the items you need first near the top*

## A sample kit list

- Kitbag, rucksack or holdall
- Sleeping bag
- Sheet liner for sleeping bag
- Anorak/waterproofs
- Wellington boots
- Hike boots
- Warm sweater, jumper/sweatshirt (essential even in summer months)
- T-shirt or similar
- Trousers or shorts
- Spare underclothes and spare socks (packed in a plastic bag)
- Nightwear – pyjamas or tracksuit for sleeping
- Shoes and spare pair of trainers, plimsolls, sandals or flip-flops
- Swimwear and towel
- Wool hat
- Scarf
- Gloves
- Sun hat, sun protection cream, sunglasses
- Handkerchiefs or tissues
- Towels
- Tea towel
- Personal washing requirements – soap, flannel, toothbrush, toothpaste, comb or hairbrush
- Personal medicines
- Two unbreakable plates, one bowl
- Unbreakable mug
- Cutlery – knife, fork, spoon and teaspoon
- Torch and spare batteries
- Individual groundsheet (if you don't have a full-size one to fit the tent)

## Choosing a rucksack

When it comes to rucksacks, there's a staggering amount of choice in terms of size, price and features, but there are two key considerations. Firstly, think about the purpose: will you be heading off for six months in the Himalayas or just spending afternoons walking? Secondly, think about the extent of use: consider spending more for a top brand, which will be more comfortable to wear as well as more durable.

In terms of size, the lightest rucksack is a hydration pack – basically a water bottle plus a small compartment, often worn by cyclists and fell runners. A day pack is the next largest, generally around 15 litres, with enough space for a coat, jumper and lunch – ideal for a day trip. A multi-day pack is 30 litres or more. An alpine pack is up to 60 litres, and generally tall and thin in proportions so as to reduce inconvenience when climbing. An expedition pack, for when it gets serious, is up to 100 litres. If travelling with a rucksack, don't be ashamed to use a version fitted with wheels so that it can be dragged rather carried at stations and airports.

One of the most important features is the back system – basically the way the rucksack is attached. 'Standard' is the system used for the lightest pack; the pack is next to the body and there is normally some padding or cushioning. The next category is 'Air-Cooled'; this allows a gap between you and the pack, preventing you from becoming hot and sticky! 'Adjustable' is the most sophisticated, allowing you to create your own bespoke system, distributing the weight according to your body's ability to carry it.

# WATER CARRIERS

Having easy access to plenty of cool drinking water is vital for all outdoor activities. There's a wide choice of containers available, from a simple plastic bottle to a high-tech hydration system. What you choose will be determined by the amount you're prepared to spend, and also the space available.

A good dependable item is the aluminium carrier, which normally holds half a litre and comes with a karabiner that can clip to your belt or pack. These cannot be easily damaged and will protect your precious water supplies. If weight and convenience are your biggest considerations, then a foldable foil or plastic bag might be a better option – this can be collapsed after the water has been drunk. Finally a hydration pack or water bladder is the most sophisticated system; this comes with a hose and mouthpiece, allowing you to take on water without breaking your stride.

# CAMP LAYOUT AND PLANNING

Finding the perfect spot to set up your tent is easy enough if you know what to look for and what to avoid. Just make sure you're not the last to turn up – you may end up pitching your tent in a soggy ditch.

## Finding a site

Finding a good campsite can make the difference between a trip that's merely satisfactory rather than really great. There are plenty of sites around and a quick search on the internet or using a guide book will reveal a whole range of sites from small and basic to the large and commercial (with lots of on-site activities). Booking in advance is strongly advised, and the earlier you book the more likely you are to get the site you want.

Whatever you choose to go for, you'll need some basic amenities – a good water supply, toilets and waste disposal are the fundamental requirements. In addition to this you might want to make sure that there are showers, a shop close by or easy access to transport links.

When you arrive you'll be allocated a 'pitch', or you might be able to choose your own. If possible you want one that'll offer protection from the wind, is high enough so that it won't get flooded if the weather turns, and isn't too near areas of the site that are likely to get noisy. You'll also want your pitch to be as flat as possible so that you don't all end

up rolling down to one end of the tent during the night. Try not to put your tent under trees, as you'll be dripped upon long after the rain has stopped, and in extreme conditions the tree could be struck by lightning or the wind might blow branches down.

# CAMP LAYOUT

Think carefully about the location of your tents and other facilities; if you're travelling in a large group and you know how many tents there will be, it's a good idea to sketch out an ideal plan before you arrive.

Depending on how you intend to cater for yourself you may need an area for cooking. Again you should find somewhere that's sheltered from the wind and is flat so that your stove will be stable and unlikely to be blown over whilst in use. You should also position the stove a reasonable distance from your tent, so as to avoid any mishaps.

A simple shelter such as a gazebo can provide good shelter in wet conditions and a table will ensure that you can cook comfortably and keep your food well away from the mud.

If you're lucky enough to be allowed an open fire, then again ensure that it's a safe distance from the tents. Find out the direction of the prevailing wind and make sure the smoke won't be blown directly into the sleeping area. Allow at least a 25-metre exclusion zone around the fire and check there are no overhanging branches that could catch fire.

Scouts traditionally camp in a circle or horseshoe around a flag; not only does this give unity to the camp, but it also provides a sense of togetherness and safety, and allows the leader of the camp to check everything is in order at a glance.

If possible, it's good idea to have separate tents set up for stores and first aid. A first aid tent, which will provide privacy for someone who needs to recuperate, should be next to the adult leader tent to ensure that the medical supplies are kept safe.

Toilets and washing are essential to the well-being of campers. Young campers especially won't use the facilities if they're dirty, wet and dark. It's wise to take your own supply of loo roll. If you have a portable loo or latrines, put these downwind of the rest of the camp, and, if possible, behind trees or rocks for privacy.

Finally, if there are children at the camp and there are areas of water, ensure that play areas are clearly marked out and that children are carefully supervised. Familiarise yourself with the local life-saving procedures and equipment.

# FINDING WATER

To stay healthy it's important to closely monitor your water intake and insure that it's fit to drink. In a temperate climate an adult will need seven pints or four litres per day. Here are three easy ways to find it.

## 1 Rainwater

In most areas the rain will provide you with a pure source of water. If you use a tarp or tent to sleep in then rainwater collection will be a valuable by-product of its use. Make sure your tarp is clean and not coated in a waterproofing solution that could taint the water. Also check the canopy above for toxic plants through which the rain could be filtering. Provide a low point to channel the water and leave a container under the drips. Alternatively, any piece of waterproof material can be used and set up to provide a huge surface area to catch every single drop.

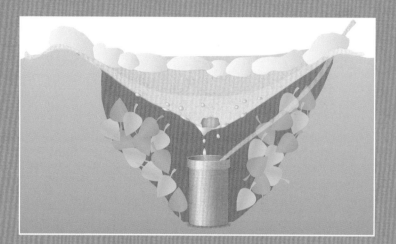

## 2 Transpiration

In sunlight trees give off water through their leaves; this is called transpiration. Use transparent polythene bags to trap and collect this water by enclosing a particularly leafy branch or bundle of foliage – from a non-poisonous variety of plant – in a sunny location. Tie the bag at the top and place a small pebble in the corner of the bag to create a low point for the water to collect.

## 3 Gypsy well

If the ground's saturated underfoot, or doesn't feel that damp but has water-loving plants like reeds, ferns and mosses nearby, then the water can be accessed by digging a 'gypsy well'. Dig a hole big enough to fit a billy can or mug in until water starts to seep in. Let it fill naturally with water. Scoop this (and possibly the second filling) out, as it'll probably be dirty. The third filling should provide you with cleaner water, but this will preferably still need to be sterilised by boiling. Refine the well by lining it with reeds or similar non-poisonous plants to act as a filter, and make a lid to keep debris out.

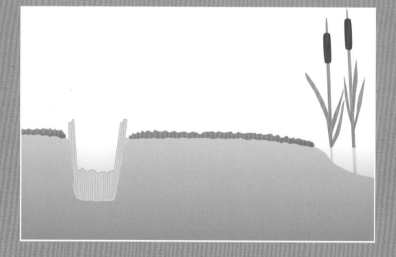

# LEAVE NO TRACE

There's a Scouting maxim about camping that goes right back to the origins of the movement: 'leave no trace'. Baden-Powell said that after a successful camp, you should 'leave nothing behind but your thanks'.

Proper disposal of waste at camp is critical for hygiene, legal compliance and the opportunity to camp again on the same site.

The first rule of waste is to make as little as possible. By planning ahead you can minimise the amount produced. For example, buy products without excess packaging and plan your catering carefully to minimise uneaten food. If you don't make waste, you don't have to dispose of it. This is doubly so of waste water (also known as 'grey water') – the less water you use, the less waste is produced.

## Types of waste at camp
Camping generates all sorts of waste. Of particular risk are:

**1 Detergents** – these are highly toxic to water life, and have long life in the soil, as well as creating visible contamination. Use sparingly and, if available, use biodegradable detergent or one with low environmental impact.

**2 Fats and greases** – these create a trap for other contaminants, are unsightly, and rapidly provide a breeding ground for bacteria and vermin. Minimise the use of oils and fats at camp when cooking, and plan diets and cooking methods appropriately.

Accident risks can arise from sharp edges, glass or chemical content in waste, aside from the basic trip hazard or 'clutter factor'. Waste also presents a significant fire hazard at camp, especially paper and plastic waste near a cooking area.

## Water and wet pits
The recommended method of water disposal is a wet pit, which first filters 'solids' out of water (like beans from washing-up water), provides a chemical trap for toxins, then finally access to aerated soils allowing natural bacteria to decontaminate the rest.

### How to make a wet pit in the ground
This method is fine if you are in, for example, a farmer's field and have asked permission first.

**1** Dig your hole. This should be at least 30cm square, and 45–60cm deep.
**2** Remove the turf carefully, place face down and keep well watered. If you can, find plastic to put it on.
**3** Once you have your hole, make a frame, weave a lattice of green branches (with holes approximately 1cm apart) and place over the hole, and finally put long grass or bracken on top.
**4** To use, simply pour the water slowly on the top of the wet pit, and the grass will filter out all the solid matter.
**5** Change the filter material regularly (at least once a day); used filter material can be burnt. If you're on a long camp, the position of the wet pit should be changed every few days.

### WARNING!
A pit is a serious hazard and needs to be clearly marked and preferably roped off. A pit should never be within 100m of a water course, lake or well.

## At the end of camp
**1** Clean your equipment before packing it away; this will make unpacking much more pleasant and prevent stubborn stains.
**2** Sort clean clothes from dirty ones, ready for washing or putting away when you get home.
**3** Dispose of waste and waste water in accordance with campsite rules.
**4** If you have dug a wet pit, remove the lattice and undergrowth from your wet pit, and fill in. Replace the turf on the top and put a 'foul ground' marker (a small cross made of sticks) in the middle to warn other campers that you have used that spot.
**5** Ensure that your campfire is completely out and that you have dowsed the embers. Even when not glowing, embers can remain very hot and have the potential to ignite any suitable tinder that comes into contact with them.
**6** If you have cut turf to make your fireplace, replace it as you found it.
**7** Walk around the whole campsite and check to ensure you have left no rubbish or equipment; be especially vigilant for pegs left in the ground.
**8** Thank the landowner or campsite manager and invite them to carry out their own inspection. This courtesy will go a long way, especially if you want to return to the same site.

# PROJECT:
# A-FRAME SHELTER

As you'd expect, an A-frame shelter resembles a letter 'A' when viewed end-on. It's one of the most popular and versatile kinds of emergency shelter as it can be built relatively quickly, can be built to any size, and is quite sturdy if constructed properly.

**Difficulty**  **Total time** Allow 1 hour +

Before you begin work on your A-frame, check that the site is suitable – for example, don't build it near an animal trail or ants' nest. Check that there aren't any dead branches above you. Think about where the sun rises and sets and the direction of the prevailing wind – you can judge the terrain and surrounding flora to help avoid an exposed position. Avoid lower ground between two high points, as cold air can collect in such places and rain run-off may be a problem.

Spend time selecting and gathering your materials first, so that you can then concentrate on building your shelter in one sustained session. To a certain extent you can improvise the foliage depending on what you find on the forest floor.

*The A-Frame is a favourite design of survival schools everywhere, but don't forget your groundsheet!*

**1** To start the frame you'll need a straight and sturdy ridge pole and two forked supports. Make sure the supports are locked together and that the ridge pole is also secured through the middle. You should be able to rest your weight on the entrance end of the ridge pole at this point. You can use a sharpened digging stick to create small depressions in the ground for the supports. Next clear any debris inside the frame and check for sharp stones. Before going further, lie down within the frame to check that you can fit inside without your head sticking out or your feet touching the ridge pole.

**3** Once the frame is finished and you have as many sticks in place as possible (this will help to support the leaf litter covering added in the next step) the thatching process can start. Utilise material such as large pieces of bark, thin twigs (from trees such as silver birch) and foliage. For the foliage, bracken leaves are excellent as they are large and commonly found, so they will help make the thatching process quick and efficient; cut bracken rather than pull it as the whole plant is easily uprooted.

**2** Now build the sides using more sticks, which should rest on the ridge pole. Use fairly straight sticks, avoid rotten ones and trim to size so that they don't exceed the ridge pole too much. This will help prevent rain running down them and on to you. If any won't stay in place, either push them into the ground, or if the ground is hard weave very thin branches or plants such as nettles between them for support; but again, don't let them stick outwards (this could funnel rain in) or inwards (you will knock them and disturb the thatch).

**4** Finally, add copious amounts of leaf litter, starting at the base of the frame and working upwards towards the apex. Using a coat or old tarp will speed up collection, and keep checking in the entrance for chinks of daylight. If there's no chance of wind and rain, a minimal covering will make a surprisingly cosy shelter. If it's going to be wet then pile up at least 30cm of leaf litter all over. Try not to scoop up soil and small debris as you gather the leaf litter, as it may fall on you during the night.

# PROJECT: TEPEE

Building a tepee is a great exercise and tremendous fun for a team of 6–12 people, who can all be engaged in the project the whole time. From cutting the wood to the final covering could take four hours. You might also like to build your own ladder to tie the top coverings.

**Difficulty**           **Total time** Allow 4 hours +

The tepee is a great project for a small team to work on together. Not only is it an excellent team-building exercise but if you make your tepee well enough, you should all be able to sleep in it for the night – a perfect outdoor adventure! Just make sure you leave enough time to build the tepee before it gets too dark.

The poles will need lashing together with rope and so you may need to refer to pages 116–123, which contain information on essential knots and lashings.

**1** First you need to decide where to construct your tepee, so find a cooperative landowner who'll allow you to thin out part of a wood or an overgrown corner of a field. To build a tepee big enough to sleep as many as ten people (with a floor of 4–5m diameter and a circumference of 12–15m), you need four long poles of roughly 6–7m in length (ideally in hazel, pollarded sweet chestnut or birch), four slightly shorter poles, and a lot of thinner hazel branches to weave and tie around the structure.

**2** Start by laying out the four long poles in a star shape, and have the upper ends crossing about 1m from the top. Measure an equal distance to the crossing from the base of each pole. Tie the poles with thickish rope in a very loose figure-of-eight-type knot.

**3** Next, you need at least two people to hold each long pole and a strong person in the middle with a forked pole about 2m long. The centre person thrusts the crossing upwards with his or her pole, while the others walk inwards until the required shape is achieved – taller is better than flatter. If you want to fly a flag on the top, fix it to the longest pole before you erect it!

**5** Using sisal string, start to weave and tie three circles of hazel, using quick square lashings and trimming off any sharp branches that might tear the covering. A light person should be able to climb up the side to secure the very top, or a ladder could be used (or made!). At this stage further short uprights could be stood between the main uprights to fill in the larger gaps. In addition the space for an entrance needs to be identified.

**4** The base of each long pole should be dug into the ground a little, and it's essential that the bases are secured to large pegs driven into the ground to prevent the tepee being blown over. Then the slightly shorter set of four poles is simply laid between the main poles, although it isn't necessary to tie them at the top.

**6** Finally, there's the task of covering the tepee with tarps or camouflaged plastic sheets, starting at the bottom and making higher pieces overlap. There's no easy guide here (covering a cone with rectangular shapes must be a mathematician's dream) and there will be plenty of overlap. If lots of people will sleep in the tepee, consider leaving a ventilation space around the bottom, although there'll be many places where air will flow between the covering sheets.

# WILD CAMPING
## IN THE UK

Wild camping is often seen as the purest form of outdoor experience. It's wonderful to wake up and unzip the door of your tent to be greeted by a spectacular view of mountains and glens.

## Planning

You're close to nature, away from man-made environments and free to enjoy the countryside first-hand. But wild camping doesn't necessarily mean there are no rules. To avoid damage to habitats and injury to wildlife, it's important to plan your expedition.

While wild camping, of course, is about freedom, it's equally important not to be complacent. As it's illegal to camp in England and Wales without permission of the landowner, you should make every effort to locate the owner (normally the local farmer) before pitching your tent. However, in more remote areas it's acknowledged that this isn't always possible, in which case you should follow these simple rules:

- Avoid open fires.
- Don't travel in large groups.
- Be as unobtrusive as possible and if possible stay out of line of sight.
- Keep noise to a minimum.
- Pitch late and leave early.
- Stay for a maximum of one night in any one spot.
- Don't disturb wildlife or livestock.
- Leave no litter.
- Don't dig holes except to bury human waste.
- Take all food scraps home with you.

## The Countryside Code

Whenever you're out exploring the countryside, always adhere to the Countryside Code:

- Be safe – plan ahead and follow any signs.
- Leave gates and property as you find them.
- Protect plants and animals, and take your litter home.
- Keep dogs under close control.
- Consider other people.

For full details go to:
www.countrysideaccess.gov.uk for England
www.ccw.org.uk for Wales
www.outdooraccess-scotland.com for Scotland
www.nidirect.gov.uk/the-countryside-code for Northern Ireland

A good compromise is to find a campsite with a minimum of modern facilities and therefore the feel of wild camping, without the uncertainty. An excellent guide to these is www.pitchup.com/wild-camping which allows you to search sites not only by location and amenities, but also by their relatively unspoiled atmosphere.

# HIKING AND TREKKING

Carrying your kit on your back is harder work than arriving by car, but for the sense of freedom and adventure it's well worth the extra effort.

Although hiking to your campsite may not be to everyone's taste, a lot of people look upon it as part and parcel of their camping adventure – and if you don't want to cycle, or want the freedom to take to footpaths, what greener way could there be to go on holiday? Don't be too over-ambitious at first; if you aren't used to hiking with your home on your back then start with shorter routes and build up gradually as you gain more experience and become familiar with your abilities.

Once you're comfortable with hiking for reasonable distances, you may want to go to the next level and try your hand (or more appropriately your feet) at trekking – undertaking a long journey on foot in an area where transport is unavailable. Commonly trekking involves walking for a number of days on often uncharted paths in challenging environments that are likely to be hilly or very remote.

You need to have a reasonable level of fitness to go trekking, and should have good skills in navigation and self-reliance due to the lack of immediate assistance should things not go according to plan.

The equipment you carry will also need to be of good quality and suitable for the environment in which you intend to use it. Remember that you're going to be self-sufficient for several days at a time, so your kit may need to be more comprehensive than for more conventional camping, and include at the very least a stove, sleeping bag and dry clothes, as well as your food and water.

For the novice trekker, travelling with an experienced guide either as part of a commercial venture or with a club or society is a good, safe way to undertake your first trek. Later, when you've gained more experience, you may wish to plan your own trips, but be sure that you let the local authorities know of your intended route and the estimated time that it'll take to get there. In this way the alert will be raised if you go missing. Also, it's better to go as part of a group, as this spreads the burden of carrying kit and is safer.

You should adopt a policy of 'leave no trace' when in remote areas, to avoid damage to the environment. It's safer for flora and fauna and means the next person to travel that way will get as much enjoyment from the unspoiled surroundings as you did.

# WHERE TO CAMP

When it comes to wild camping, weather conditions, environment and even laws differ depending on your destination, so make sure you're prepared .

## Scotland

In Scotland, where the laws are more relaxed and wild camping is permitted, the best and most beautiful places to seek out are the Highlands, areas around Loch Lomond, Glencoe and the Cairngorms. The Mar Estate near Braemar is also an excellent location, although be careful not to stray into Balmoral!

Of course, while the legal framework in Scotland is more conducive to wild camping, the insect population isn't so welcoming – midges are a pest to wild campers, so avoid camping close to water or other known midge haunts.

The fact that wild camping is legal in Scotland without the permission of the landowner is due to a ground-breaking piece of legislation, the Land Reform (Scotland) Act 2003. This right is granted on the basis that you follow a clear code of practice, which includes camping away from houses and roadsides (which isn't really in the spirit of wild camping anyway). You aren't trespassing on land as long as you follow the code, which can be found in full at www.outdooraccess-scotland.com.

Another option is to choose a wild campsite, such as the Red Squirrel campsite in Glencoe, which is popular among climbers of Ben Nevis and its lofty neighbours. Some good rural campsites include East Grange, Elgin; Lickisto, Isle of Harris; Ledgowan, Achnasheen; and Adventure in the Meadow, Gorebridge.

## Ireland and Northern Ireland

Wild camping in Ireland is possible, although it's illegal without permission. Always seek permission from the landowner and check the weather forecast first; rain is part of life in Ireland, and it can be particularly damp in low-lying areas.

Regarding good campsites, try Beech Grove Camping Park, Killarney, in the south, or Sperrin Mountains Campsite, Omagh, in the north. In Northern Ireland you're also able to camp by permit at the 'touring in the woods sites', which are operated by the Northern Irish Forest Service.

The wild camping fraternity is never short of an opinion. For some specific advice, or to join the conversation and make recommendations of your own, visit www.wildcamping.co.uk

## England

There are some specific areas in England to avoid when it comes to wild camping: these include National Trust land and National Parks. High up in the Lake District and Peak District are obvious temptations to wild campers, but again the same conditions apply – speak to the landowner first. Fires (and all naked flames) should be avoided in wooded areas and on dry moorland.

The only exception to the general rule banning wild camping in England and Wales is Dartmoor, where you may camp for up to two nights in the same place as long as you're a minimum of 100m from a road, and not in an enclosure or a restricted area.

Good campsites with a wild feel in England include Jubilee Park Farm, Winkleigh, Devon; Puffin Campsite, Bridlington; Southern Bells, Lingfield; Chester Lakes, Chester; and Moorlands Caravan Park, Kingsmead Centre, Cullompton, Devon.

## Wales

Wilder campsites in Wales include North Lodge, Boncath, Pembrokeshire; Cwmduad, Carmarthenshire; Greenways, Swansea; Bwlchgwyn Farm, Fairbourne, Gwynedd; and Larkhill, Cwmduad.

# CARBON-NEUTRAL CAMPING

'Carbon neutral' is a fashionable phrase in the world of camping, but what does it actually mean, and is it truly possible to go carbon-neutral camping?

Essentially it's about leaving a zero carbon footprint, offsetting any carbon emissions by undertaking activities that cancel these out (or by buying carbon credits). Many campsites are now proving their sustainable credentials by running programmes of environmentally friendly activities that offset the greenhouse gas released by your travel, heating and other activities.

## Measures include
- Cycling to the campsite, or at least making use of public transport to minimise carbon emissions.
- Taking part in tree planting.
- Reusing waste water for plants and flowers.
- Using only energy-efficient LED lighting.
- Using only sites powered by photovoltaic solar panels.
- Ensuring all buildings are well insulated to prevent heat loss.
- Fitting aerators on taps to reduce water usage.
- Using biodegradable cleaning products.
- Making use of recycling centres.
- Shopping for, eating and drinking locally sourced products.

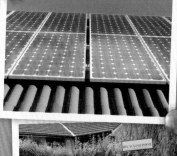

Of course, the sites you visit may not be as green as you are, so the onus is on you to lead by example, to take as many of these steps as possible yourself, and to lobby campsite owners to follow suit.

# ADVERSE CAMPING CONDITIONS

There's no point in getting worked up about bad weather; it's just a case of sitting it out. As Henry Longfellow once said: 'The best thing one can do when it's raining is to let it rain.'

## Camping in the rain

Be prepared for rain if you camp for longer than two or three days – even in the summer months it's almost guaranteed. If you absolutely have to pitch your tent in the rain then set up a tarpaulin over your tent and work beneath it. Pitch your tent on high ground so rain won't run down into it. Always put the outer part of the tent up first, unless your tent instructions specifically say otherwise. You can pitch the tarpaulin over the top of your tent to keep the worst of the rain off the tent itself. If you have a separate groundsheet then make sure it's kept well inside the tent and that the lip isn't sticking out, or else it will collect rain. Keep clothes bags and equipment away from the sides of the tent – if anything touches the walls of the tent, water will be able to seep in.

Remember to take a rain poncho, lots of plastic bags (pack your clothing and bedding in plastic bags before packing them into your rucksack), a change of clothes, and a pack of cards or a good book for an afternoon or evening indoors.

## Camping in hot weather

Where possible try and pitch your tent in the shade – particularly in the morning, so you're not woken by hot, bright sunlight too early.

Check the direction of the prevailing wind and pitch your tent in the same direction so the wind flows through, providing cooling ventilation. During the day, open up the tent as much as possible. Take on plenty of water throughout the day.

## Camping in high wind

Most family tents are designed to withstand a certain amount of wind. However, speeds over 30mph can cause damage. Please also remember that pitching a tent in the wind is extremely difficult, and potentially dangerous. If there's an option it's always best to wait until the conditions improve. Remember the tent has no aerodynamic qualities until it's fully pitched. Only you can make a proper assessment of the risks, but be especially mindful of overhanging or rotten branches that could fall in high winds.

## Camping in the cold

If you're embarking on a camping trip more ambitious than a week at the seaside in July, then you need to think carefully about protecting yourself against sudden or sustained drops in temperature.

# THUNDER AND LIGHTNING

As many as 60 people are struck by lightning in the UK each year. It's important to understand the reasons why and to do your best not to be one of the statistics.

The first signs of a storm are usually quite obvious – a rumble of thunder, for example. But the sound seeming quite distant should be of no reassurance, since a lightning strike can reach up to a ten-mile radius. In addition you should time the delay between the thunder and lightning – a gap of less than 30 seconds spells danger.

## Taking action

If you're on water, get to shore as quickly as you can, as water's an efficient conductor of electricity. If you're outdoors, seek shelter immediately – ideally in a house or other permanent structure, but otherwise in a car. A shed or tent isn't safe enough, and never shelter beneath a tree. If there really is no shelter at all, find a low place and assume the crash position, with your head between your legs, crouching down and balancing on your heels to avoid too much contact with the earth.

## Do not

- Use an umbrella
- Use a mobile phone
- Hold a golf club
- Shelter beneath a tree
- Leave your shelter too early – there's still a danger up to half an hour after the thunderstorm is over, and, yes, lightning can strike the same place, or the same person, twice.

# COLD-WEATHER EQUIPMENT

A cheap tent won't feel so much of a bargain on a windy Scottish hillside with broken poles and no shelter for miles. Likewise, your sleeping bag should be appropriate to the conditions. Most sleeping bags have a minimum temperature marked on the packaging or labels. Check this when buying your gear.

## Heating

The only safe source of heat in a tent is either your own body or someone else's. Lives have been saved by people huddling together for warmth. Don't light a fire or stove inside a tent, or drag in a barbecue – apart from the fire risk, these generate deadly carbon monoxide fumes that will become trapped in the tent.

## Food and drink

As your body is the key heat source, you need to ensure you use the right fuel. In cold weather your body needs sugars to generate heat. Ensure you eat plenty of butter and pasta, and drink hot tea or other hot drinks (especially before going to bed).

## Sleeping bag

To save money, you can use one sleeping bag inside another to improve the insulation, but think about the weight if you're hiking, and check with an expert (or knowledgeable shopkeeper) that your combination will be sufficiently warm. You'll also need a good ground mat to prevent contact with the cold ground. Sleeping bag liners are available that are lighter and take up less space.

## Clothing

Most of your heat will be lost through your head and extremities, so wear a hat (even in bed if necessary) as well as gloves, scarf and multiple pairs of socks. Don't be too proud to use a hot water bottle, which you should place at the foot of your sleeping bag some time before turning in. Beware of packing your feet too tightly, however – it's better to trap a layer of heat rather than packing your feet too tightly into your boots (which can also cut off or impair your blood circulation). In addition wear light, wicking layers close to the skin beneath your other winter clothing. Black clothing will absorb more heat.

## Storms and floods

Most of the time the weather in this part of the world follows a fairy predictable pattern, depending on the particular area and time of year. But it's always a mistake to take it for granted, and warnings of severe weather should always be taken seriously.

Thunderstorms can seemingly appear out of nowhere, even on a sunny day. In the right conditions, fluffy cumulus clouds can soon build up into towering cumulonimbus clouds 10 miles high or more. The air below the clouds may be warm, but at the top the temperature is freezing. Inside them air currents rise and fall rapidly, carrying water vapour that quickly condenses into heavy rain.

If a downpour is very heavy or prolonged, the water may not be able to soak away in the normal fashion. Instead it builds up on the surface, washing away soil, boulders, trees and other vegetation, causing rivers and reservoirs to overflow, damaging buildings and flooding into low-lying areas.

Flash floods can turn dry river courses, gullies and small streams into raging torrents in minutes, even though the storm that caused them is some distance away. Always be cautious when travelling in areas where flash floods are known to occur.

## Flood safety

- If you think there's danger of flooding, get to high ground or the upper floors of a building as quickly as possible.
- Do not try to walk or wade through flood water. It's very easy to underestimate the depth and power of the flow, and impossible to know what objects may be under the water. If the water's above your ankles, it's too deep to cross.
- Never attempt to travel by car along flooded roads. If the car stalls, get out and climb on to higher ground. Most cars can be swept away in as little as 60cm of water.
- If you have time, take supplies of drinking water, food, a torch, matches and warm clothing with you.
- Once you find a safe place, stay there until the flood water drops or you're rescued.

## Hypothermia

**Hypothermia occurs when a person's body temperature drops below 35°C. In this state excessive shivering, confusion, slurred speech and clumsiness will result. If you suspect someone's becoming hypothermic you should warm them up gradually – not too quickly. Ideally this means getting them to a warm shelter, but at the very least they should huddle up with others, drink something warm and be dressed in dry clothes. Seek emergency medical attention. An early sign of frostbite is a whitening of the skin that doesn't return to normal colour after applying pressure. Seek immediate emergency medical attention.**

# NAVIGATION SKILLS

Scouts pride themselves on their sense of direction, but even we struggle without the right knowledge, equipment and training. The travel writer D. Francis Morgan once said: 'Map and compass are the chief tools of the explorer, but they are of little use to the person who does not know how to use them.' You can now add GPS to this list, but, once again, equipment alone isn't always the answer.

# MAP READING

Without a map, the world is only as wide as the eye can see. However if you have a good map, drawn to scale, and you know how to read it, you'll be able to 'see' for many miles in every direction. A map gives us an eagle-eyed view of the world.

## Drawn to scale

A map is a two-dimensional (flat) representation of three-dimensional land, looking from directly above. Every Ordnance Survey (OS) map is drawn to scale and the two most common scales used are 1:25,000 or 1:50,000 – this means that a 1cm distance measured on the map is equivalent to 250m or 500m respectively when scaled up to full size. The map will have the scale printed on it.

The phrase 'drawn to scale' simply refers to the fact that the map would perfectly match the ground covered if it were to be enlarged to the same size as the landscape. Beware of any map that is not drawn to scale (for example one drawn by hand). Although better than no map at all, it is likely to give you inaccurate impressions of the land around you. Using this, you may embark on a journey that will take much longer than anticipated, and landmarks may not appear as early as you expected them, if at all.

A good-quality map, therefore, is essential, as is a map carrier to prevent it from getting soggy in the rain.

## Measuring distance

Take your Ordnance Survey map and familiarise yourself with the scale. For example, check the distance between the grid lines. Does it represent 1km, or more or less? This information will be provided on the map.

Now find your starting point and your end point. Just by assessing the distance between these points, you should, with the aid of the grid lines, be able to make a reasonably good estimate at this stage.

To measure the exact distance along a path, take a piece of straight paper and a pencil and mark each straight section of the path on the paper. If you come to a bend, twist the paper to measure the next straight section, and so on, until you have arrived at your destination and measured the whole distance. You should now have a series of marks along the straight edge of the paper. Take these and measure the total length from your first pencil mark to you last pencil mark along the scale line at the bottom of the map. From this, you will be able to calculate the exact length of your journey.

**1:25 000**

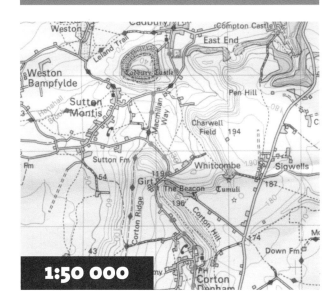

**1:50 000**

# GRID REFERENCES

Grid references are the co-ordinates used to identify a particular geographical location on a map. They could be used to identify the end point of a hike for example, or pinpoint the whereabouts of a casualty in an emergency situation.

To find a location on a map a set of reference letters and figures are given. The UK is divided into 100km squares, each with a unique two-letter code. Some maps will run across more than one of the 100km lettered squares, and in order to identify these it's important that you read the two-letter code(s) printed on the map, either in the corner of the map itself and/or in the legend (the key).

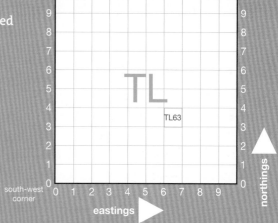

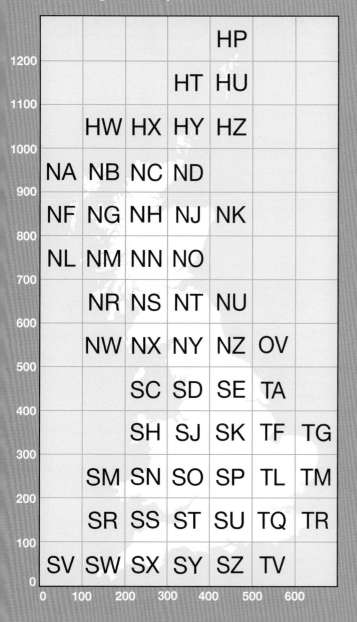

Each 100km square is then divided into numbered 1km squares, shown as blue lines on the map. These numbers start from the bottom left-hand corner of the 100km square. The kilometre numbering is printed on the sides of the map and at regular intervals within it.

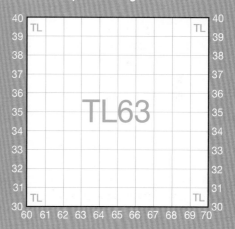

To be able to accurately reference a location/feature on the map, the 1km square should be further divided into 10 to get to 100m accuracy. Note that these lines aren't shown on the map but have to be estimated – halving the square, halving again and then guessing how close the feature is to these divisions is a good method. Therefore a full six-figure grid reference will be (for instance) TM 625 333. Notice that the horizontal numbers ('eastings') are quoted first and the vertical numbers ('northings') second. If it helps, think of it as going along the corridor and then up the stairs.

This type of reference will be accurate to approximately 100m. Modern satellite navigation devices using the Global Positioning System (GPS) will normally be more accurate and give grid reference numbers to eight figures, ie to within 10m.

# CONTOURS

Lines called contours are used to represent the undulations of the land. These are drawn on the map in a light brown colour. They connect points at the same height (above sea level) and are either 5m (1:25,000) or 10m (1:50,000) apart. The closer the contour lines are together, the steeper the slope.

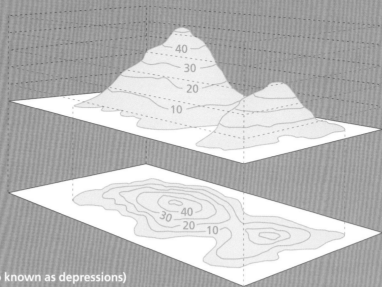

## Highs and lows

Hills (also known as elevations) and valleys (also known as depressions) can significantly affect your journey time. Although the distance will look the same on the map, it is highly likely that, because of the gradient, it will take you a longer to cover. To help gauge how long this will be, we use something called 'Naismith's rule' which says that for every 10 metres of height climbed, an extra minute should be added to your walking time.

### Hill

A hill is an elevated land mass that rises above the surrounding area. There is some controversy as to when a hill becomes a mountain, but it is generally agreed in the UK that any hill higher than 600m is classified as a mountain.

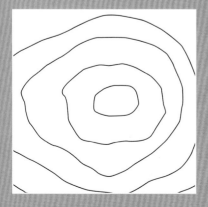

### Ridge

A ridge is a series of connected mountains that form a crest, usually at high altitude. Once a summit has been achieved, it is sometimes possible to walk along a ridge to reach the summit of an adjoining mountain.

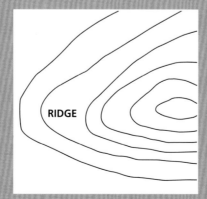

RIDGE

### Valley

Also known as a dale, canyon or gorge, a valley is a depression in the landscape that slopes downwards before rising back up again. A valley is usually V-shaped if formed by a river, or U-shaped if formed by a glacier during an ice age.

## Setting a map

It's a good idea when navigating with a map to align the map with the landscape. This is known as 'setting' a map. First, find a feature or landmark and stand next to it. Mark where you're standing on the map (you can use your finger). Hold the map parallel to the ground and then rotate the map so that other features and landmarks on the map begin to line up with the actual ones you can see. The map is now 'set' to the land, although not as accurately as it would be using a compass.

## Map symbols

Features in the landscape are depicted as symbols. Not all symbols are used on all maps, so you should check the key on each Ordnance Survey map. The symbols below are typical of what you would find on an Ordnance Survey map. Take some time to familiarise youself with these as it will make reading a map so much quicker and easier, especially when out walking.

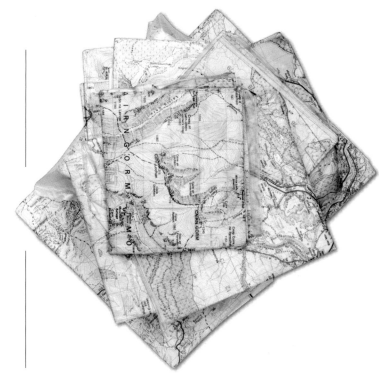

### ROADS AND PATHS

| | |
|---|---|
| M I or A 6(M) | Motorway |
| A 35 | Dual carriageway |
| A 30 | Main road |
| B 3074 | Secondary road |
| | Narrow road with passing places |
| | Road under construction |
| | Road generally more than 4 m wide |
| | Road generally less than 4 m wide |
| | Other road, drive or track, fenced or unfenced |
| | Path |

### RAILWAYS

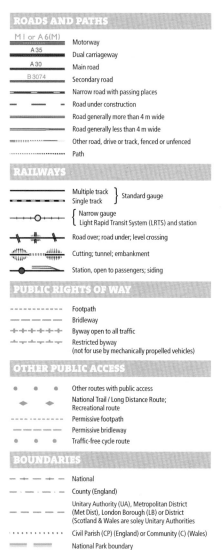

| | |
|---|---|
| Multiple track / Single track | Standard gauge |
| | Narrow gauge / Light Rapid Transit System (LRTS) and station |
| | Road over; road under; level crossing |
| | Cutting; tunnel; embankment |
| | Station, open to passengers; siding |

### PUBLIC RIGHTS OF WAY

| | |
|---|---|
| | Footpath |
| | Bridleway |
| | Byway open to all traffic |
| | Restricted byway (not for use by mechanically propelled vehicles) |

### OTHER PUBLIC ACCESS

| | |
|---|---|
| | Other routes with public access |
| | National Trail / Long Distance Route; Recreational route |
| | Permissive footpath |
| | Permissive bridleway |
| | Traffic-free cycle route |

### BOUNDARIES

| | |
|---|---|
| | National |
| | County (England) |
| | Unitary Authority (UA), Metropolitan District (Met Dist), London Borough (LB) or District (Scotland & Wales are soley Unitary Authorities |
| | Civil Parish (CP) (England) or Community (C) (Wales) |
| | National Park boundary |

### ARCHAEOLOGICAL AND HISTORICAL

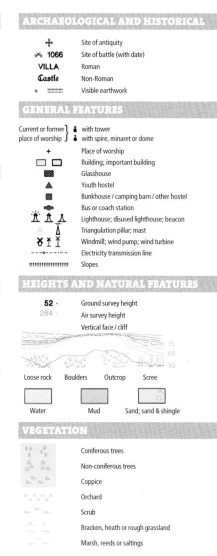

| | |
|---|---|
| | Site of antiquity |
| 1066 | Site of battle (with date) |
| VILLA | Roman |
| Castle | Non-Roman |
| * | Visible earthwork |

### GENERAL FEATURES

| | |
|---|---|
| Current or former place of worship | with tower |
| | with spire, minaret or dome |
| + | Place of worship |
| | Building; important building |
| | Glasshouse |
| | Youth hostel |
| | Bunkhouse / camping barn / other hostel |
| | Bus or coach station |
| | Lighthouse; disused lighthouse; beacon |
| | Triangulation pillar; mast |
| | Windmill; wind pump; wind turbine |
| | Electricity transmission line |
| | Slopes |

### HEIGHTS AND NATURAL FEATURES

| | |
|---|---|
| 52 · | Ground survey height |
| 284 · | Air survey height |
| | Vertical face / cliff |

| Loose rock | Boulders | Outcrop | Scree |
|---|---|---|---|

| Water | Mud | Sand; sand & shingle |
|---|---|---|

### VEGETATION

| | |
|---|---|
| | Coniferous trees |
| | Non-coniferous trees |
| | Coppice |
| | Orchard |
| | Scrub |
| | Bracken, heath or rough grassland |
| | Marsh, reeds or saltings |

### ACCESS LAND

| | |
|---|---|
| | Access land boundary and tint |
| | Access land in woodland area |
| | Access information point |
| DANGER AREA | Firing and test ranges in the area. Danger! Observe warning notices. Visit www.access.mod.uk for information |
| MANAGED ACCESS | Access permitted within managed controls for example, local byelaws. Visit www.access.mod.uk for information |

### TOURIST AND LEISURE INFORMATION

| | |
|---|---|
| P | Parking |
| i | Information centre |
| V | Visitor centre |
| | Forestry Commission visitor centre |
| PC | Public conveniences |
| | Telephone; roadside telephone; emergency telephone |
| | Camp site; caravan site |
| | Preserved railway |
| | Public house |
| | Walks |
| | Cycle trail |
| | Mountain bike trail |
| | Cycle hire |
| | Viewpoint |
| | Picnic site |
| | Water activities |
| | Slipway |
| | Nature reserve |
| | Fishing |
| | Cathedral / Abbey |
| | Museum |
| | Castle / Fort |
| | Building of historic interest |
| | Heritage centre |
| | National Trust |
| | English Heritage |
| | Historic Scotland |

# USING A COMPASS

A compass is an instrument with a magnetised needle that points to magnetic north. Today, in one form or another, compasses are used on land, at sea and in the air to help people to specify direction.

Modern compasses come in different shapes and sizes; indeed, a piece of suspended magnetic ore (which always comes to rest in a north–south direction) was used many centuries ago as a primitive form of compass.

## Air-damped compass

This is the simplest and cheapest form of compass and does little more than indicate the approximate direction of magnetic north. It takes a long time to stabilise and the slightest movement makes the needle move. This compass should never be used for any sort of hike or expedition.

## Simple map-setting compass

This is a liquid-filled compass with only magnetic north marked on it and can be clipped to the side of a map. It's useful for positioning a map until whatever's actually in front of you is in front of you on the map. This can only be approximate, as there's no allowance for magnetic variation – meaning the difference between magnetic north and grid (map) north (this is explained in more detail later).

## Prismatic compass

This is a more expensive type of compass with a prism that enables a compass bearing to be taken while sighting your objective. It can be more accurate than other compasses but more complicated, and should only be used once the basic principles of map and compass work have been mastered.

## Silva-type compass

This consists of a magnetised needle suspended in an alcohol-filled housing. The liquid helps to 'dampen' movement of the needle, enabling it to be read more quickly than an air-damped compass. The compass housing has etched orienting lines and an orienting arrow, while the baseplate has map scales and an arrow for direction of travel etched on to it. This is the compass of choice for hiking and expedition-type activities because it allows bearings – an accurate method of determining direction – to be worked out.

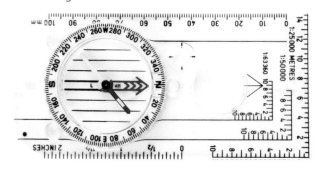

As you can see, it's possible to have varying qualities of compass depending upon what job they have to do and ultimately, of course, how much you pay for them!

## Anatomy of a compass

The image below is of a classic Silva compass, commonly used for orienteering and hiking. It is worth familiarising yourself with every aspect of the compass and try using it in a known area first. There are a potentially baffling number of marks and measurements – none of which should be first encountered while lost in the cold and rain. The most important feature is the direction of travel arrow, as the entire point of a compass, if used correctly is to point you in the right direction.

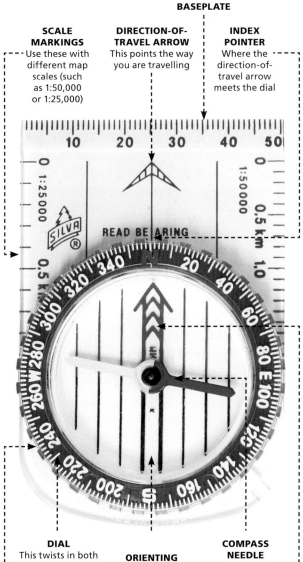

**BASEPLATE**

**SCALE MARKINGS**
Use these with different map scales (such as 1:50,000 or 1:25,000)

**DIRECTION-OF-TRAVEL ARROW**
This points the way you are travelling

**INDEX POINTER**
Where the direction-of-travel arrow meets the dial

**DIAL**
This twists in both directions, and is marked with the cardinal points (north, south, east and west) as well as the degrees

**HOUSING**
The housing encases the dial, arrow, lines and needle

**ORIENTING LINES**
These are normally red and black and are also printed on the bottom of the compass

**COMPASS NEEDLE**
Usually red and white – the red end points north

**ORIENTING ARROW**
This is a red arrow printed on the bottom of the compass; it will turn when you twist the dial

# HOW TO USE A COMPASS

This procedure will help you to understand the basic function of a compass with a rotating dial. Try experimenting by turning your body and then the dial to face the other compass points.

**1** With the compass level, and the direction-of-travel arrow pointing away from you, twist the dial so that the 'N' and the red orienting arrow line up with the direction-of-travel arrow.

**2** With the compass flat in your palm, turn your whole body (the needle will turn with you) until the needle of the compass is aligned with the north position.

**3** Turn 90 degrees to the right. Everything should now point north, except that the red needle appears to be pointing west; in fact it's pointing north (you have changed direction by moving).

**4** Twist the dial to ensure the letter 'N' and the orienting arrow once again line up with the needle. The letter 'E' is now lined up with your direction of travel, indicating that east is in front of you.

# THE THREE NORTHS

When working with a map and compass, there are three different 'norths' to be considered. Fortunately, in the UK, for practical purposes, we only have to consider and work with two of them.

## True north

Each day the Earth rotates about its axis once. The ends of the axis are the true North and true South Poles.

## Grid north

The grid lines, pointing to grid north, on Ordnance Survey maps divide Great Britain into 100km sections. They're then further subdivided into 1km squares, east of an imaginary zero point in the Atlantic Ocean, west of Cornwall. The majority of grid lines are 1.5° west of true North and are therefore useful lines to refer to when taking bearings.

## Magnetic north

A compass needle points to the magnetic North Pole. Unfortunately, however, this isn't in the same position as the true North Pole. The magnetic North Pole is currently located in the Baffin Island region of Canada and, from the UK, is west of true north. The difference between grid north and magnetic north is known as

the magnetic variation, and its value can be found in the orientation panel or margin of an Ordnance Survey map.

As true north is only about 1.5° off grid north, the difference is so small that it's normally disregarded and only grid north and magnetic north are used.

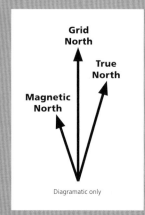

## Magnetic variation

The difference between magnetic north and true north is caused by the North and South Poles not being directly 'opposite' one another. The lines of the Earth's magnetic field don't run in a regular pattern, as they're affected by other local magnetic forces and the magnetic pole is always on the move. Some of these

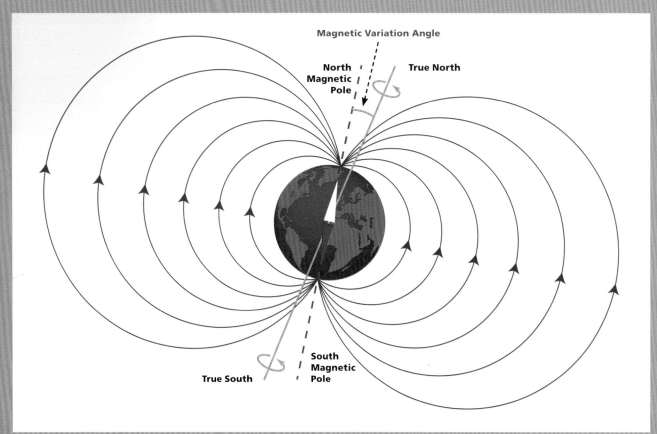

lines of magnetic variation are east of true north and others west of true north. Between the east and west lines there's a line of zero magnetic variation where the compass does point to true north – this line is known as the agonic line, currently running through eastern Canada, the United States of America and South America.

However, not only does the magnetic variation change as you move across the Earth's surface, but it also changes with time. It's important to check the magnetic variation regularly, and this can be found on a map's orientation panel or margin. Remember also to check the year the map was printed, as a map that is around 20 years old could be several degrees out. In fact, the magnetic variation also varies from side to side and top to bottom on each and every map, but these details can also be found on the map.

This magnetic variation is important when combining a map and compass, as you need to convert bearings from 'map to field'. To convert grid bearings (which are indicated by a map) to magnetic bearings (as indicated by the compass pointing to magnetic north), add the current variation by turning the compass housing anti-clockwise. For example, if the current variation is 4°, a grid bearing of 122° would become 126°; this is what the dial should be set at. The reverse is true for converting a magnetic bearing to a grid bearing; you subtract the current variation. There are various ways to remember this, but perhaps the best is to reason that, since the country is always larger than the map, the grid bearing should always be made larger when working from the map to the country. Or you may prefer to remember 'from field to grid: get rid'.

For expeditions abroad, however, some parts of the world won't only have a different value, but may also be east of true north, in which case, when converting from grid to magnetic bearings, the magnetic variation should be subtracted from the compass bearing.

Deposits of iron-based minerals in the Earth's crust, large iron or steel objects, or objects which contain steel or iron, can have a very strong influence on a compass. So do not, for example, use a compass propped against a motor vehicle, or steadied on an iron fence post! Compasses are also strongly affected by the electro-magnetic fields created by power lines and electric wiring. Seemingly innocent objects like cameras, penknives, torches, ice-axes, whistles, rucksack frames, zip fasteners and wristwatches can also affect the accuracy of a compass. Find out for yourself what effect these things can have as they're brought closer to your compass.

## Caring for your compass

Though robust, a compass should be treated with the respect that a highly sensitive instrument deserves. Don't drop it or expose it to excessive heat, and keep it away from radiators and glove compartments of vehicles; otherwise the capsule could develop a bubble which, depending on its size, may impair its efficiency. Store it away from other compasses, steel and iron objects, electrical appliances and electric circuits.

## To use a compass proficiently, it's necessary to be able to:

☑ Take a bearing – determine the angle between north and the direction of an object in terms of degrees.

☑ Walk on a bearing – use a bearing to get to a destination without necessarily using a map.

☑ Set a map – use a compass to correctly position a map in order to represent what can actually be seen.

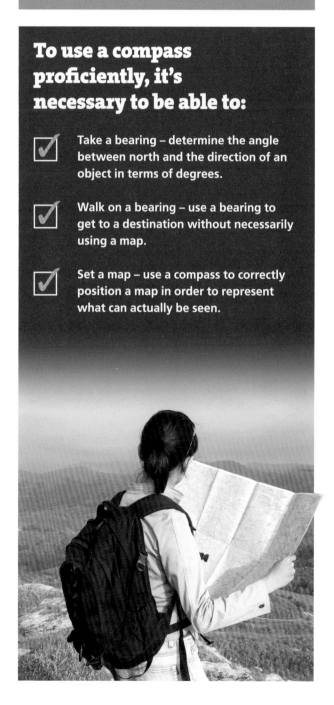

## Setting a map with a compass

This is for when you're using a map with a compass to reach a given destination, probably in unfamiliar territory.

**1** Turn the compass housing until the magnetic variation for the area is shown against the index pointer.

**2** Place the direction-of-travel arrow pointing along the vertical grid line, with the direction-of-travel arrow pointing to the top of the map.

**3** Turn the map with the compass in this position until the compass needle points to the north mark on the housing.

**4** Your map is now 'set' and you should be able to recognise actual features from your map in front of you.

However, your compass doesn't point to the grid north of your map but to magnetic north. As we've already said, the location of magnetic north varies in different parts of the world and is constantly changing. The magnetic variation throughout the UK currently ranges from 2° to 6°. The amount of variation changes every year, so check your Ordnance Survey map to work out the current value. Orientate the map by carefully turning the compass housing anti-clockwise by, for example, 4°. Turn the map again to realign the magnetic needle with the red N and the map will then be set, taking account of magnetic variation.

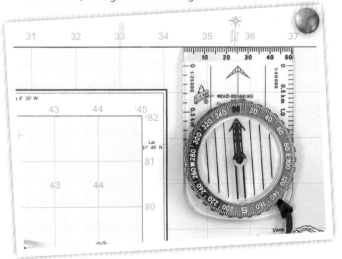

## Taking a bearing

**1** Hold the compass flat in your hand with the direction-of-travel arrow pointing towards your destination or objective.

**2** Turn the compass housing until the compass needle lines up over the orienting arrow. Ensure you use the North Pole of the needle, usually red.

**3** Read off the magnetic bearing (the number of degrees) from the mark on the compass housing indicated by the index pointer.

**4** Keep the housing in that position and check your bearing at regular intervals by lining up the needle with the orienting arrow and walking in the direction indicated by the direction-of-travel arrow.

## Walking on a bearing

This is used when you can initially see your objective or destination and don't need a map. It's important to work out a compass bearing before the situation changes (perhaps due to the weather or terrain you're in, or a delay resulting in darkness). Any of these factors may mean you can no longer see where you're aiming for and, therefore, will need to rely on the compass bearing.

**1** Turn the housing of the compass until the bearing you require is against the index pointer.

**2** Turn the compass until the needle lies over the orienting arrow.

**3** Pick out a landmark along your direction-of -ravel line and walk towards it.

**4** Check your bearing and your objective at regular intervals.

## Combining map and compass

**1** Place the compass on the map so that one long edge joins the start point and your destination, with the direction-of-travel arrow pointing towards the direction you wish to travel (the direction of the map doesn't matter for this exercise).

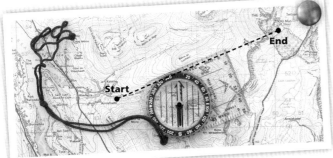

**2** Turn the compass housing until the orienting arrow points to the top of the map and the orienting lines are parallel to the grid lines.

**3** Take the compass off the map and read off the bearing at the index pointer; add (or subtract) the local magnetic variation.

**4** Turn the whole compass so that the needle comes to rest over the orienting arrow, with the red part to the north.

**5** Hold the compass in front of you, pick out a landmark along your line of travel and walk towards it.

## Avoiding obstacles

Sometimes when using a map and compass you'll come across an obstacle such as a lake or wood that cannot be crossed and you must get round them somehow. The problem is to avoid the obstacle without losing direction.

The obstacle may be bypassed by going round it by a series of right angles. Walk at 90° to your original route, count the number of paces until you clear the object. Turn 90° again, so that you are parallel with your original bearing and walk past the obstacle. Turn 90° again and walk the same number of paces. Then, finally, turn through 90° to bring yourself back on your original course.

This may seem pedantic, but it does work (providing the number of paces and turns are accurate). This can be vital if the weather suddenly worsens. An error of just 2° over a journey of 6km means that you'll miss your target by 200m. If you find yourself fog-bound and your destination is the only habitation for 20 miles around, you could be in trouble.

## Common errors

When first learning how to use a compass, there seem to be many things to take into consideration. Here are a few things that often 'go wrong':

☑ Failing to add on the magnetic variation. If the magnetic variation is, for example, 6° and you forget to add it on, you'll be 105m off course for every kilometre travelled in a straight line. This gets proportionally bigger over greater distances.

☑ Not having the direction-of-travel arrow pointing from your start to your finish. If you make this mistake you'll walk in the opposite direction (180° out).

☑ Having the orienting arrow pointing to the bottom of the map. Again, you'll walk in the opposite direction from your intended route (180° out).

☑ Not taking account of the magnetic effects of iron and steel around you, such as watches, steel buckles, cars, buried pipes, reinforced concrete, wire fences and railway lines – and even other compasses or magnetic rocks. These items might attract your compass needle in preference to magnetic North Pole, giving you an inaccurate reading. If in doubt, move away from such objects.

# WITHOUT A COMPASS

There will inevitably be occasions when you need to establish where you are, or to decide in which direction to walk, but for some reason don't have a working compass with you.

## Navigation by the sun

In the northern hemisphere the sun rises in the east, is to the south at midday, and sets in the west. So if you can see the sun and you have some idea of the time you can get a (very) general idea of directions. A more accurate method is to use a watch.

## Navigation by stick and shadow

Push an upright stick into the centre of a flat piece of ground. Mark the tip of its shadow with a stick or stone, wait about half an hour and do the same again. A line drawn between the two points will run from west to east, with the first point being west.

A more accurate method takes longer but will be more accurate. Some time before noon mark your first shadow tip as before. Using the stick as the centre point and using a piece of string, draw an arc at the distance from the stick to the shadow tip. In the afternoon, mark the exact spot where the shadow touches the arc. Now join the two points to establish the west to east line, with the morning point being west.

It is worth bearing in mind, of course, that you need plenty of sun and level ground for this method to work; if you're losing light, or if sunlight is intermittent, then it may be better to seek a different method for determining cardinal points (north, south, east and west).

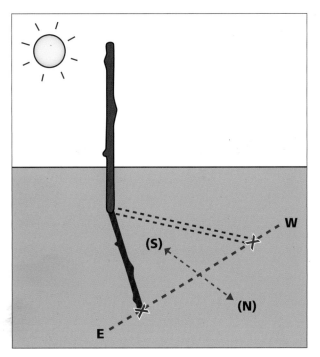

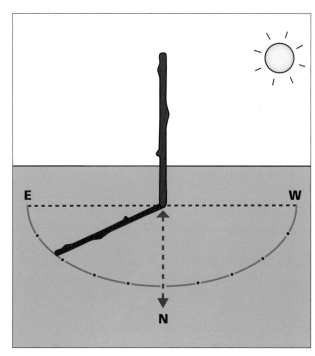

## The moon

There are lots of tricky methods for using the moon to find direction, but there's a very simple one that can help you get your rough bearings quickly. When you see a crescent moon high in the sky, join the horns in a line and then continue this line down to the ground. You'll be looking roughly south.

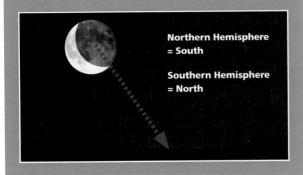

Northern Hemisphere
= South

Southern Hemisphere
= North

## Navigation by watch

First ensure your (analogue!) watch is set to local time. Then, keeping the watch face horizontal, point the hour hand as accurately as possible at the sun. An imaginary line that bisects the angle between the hour hand and the watch's 12 o'clock position (or one o'clock position in British Summer Time) will point due south.

However, this is still only an approximation, with the accuracy varying during the day by up to 35°, and is most accurate close to noon.

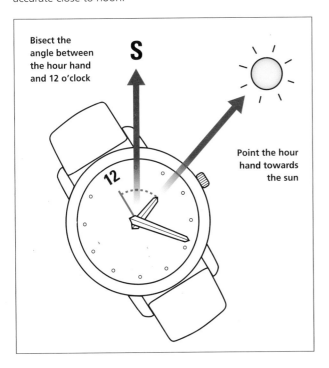

Bisect the angle between the hour hand and 12 o'clock

S

Point the hour hand towards the sun

12

# STAR GAZING

Finding direction using the stars is really easy, at least when the sky is clear. The North Star is directly above the North Pole, so if we can find it then it'll show us the way north.

Polaris

Dubhe

Merak

URSA MAJOR

To find the North Star – also called Polaris – look for the group of seven stars that comprise the constellation Ursa Major. This is more commonly known as the Plough or Big Dipper, although the shape actually looks more like a saucepan to most people. This saucepan shape never changes, although it does rotate anti-clockwise around the North Star in the sky, so it will sometimes appear on its side or even upside-down.

Now find the two stars known as the 'pointers'. If you think of the shape as a saucepan on the cooker then these pointers would be the two stars at the far right, named Dubhe and Merak.

Imagine a line connecting these two stars and then continue this imaginary line above the saucepan shape. At five times the distance you'll find the North Star: you're now looking north.

Another way of determining direction from the stars is to look for the constellation Orion, which resembles a man hunting; this is easy to spot from the three aligning stars that make up the hunter's belt. Just below the belt is a series of stars very close together that form a vertical line, known as Orion's sword. As long as this sword is near vertical, follow this downwards and it should point due south.

# NATURAL NAVIGATION

Even if you can't see the sun, it can still help. Plants tend to grow more strongly on their sunny (ie south) side. So, for example, looking at the shape of a tree canopy may help, but be wary that the prevailing wind direction may also influence plant growth.

More growth to the South

## The effect of the sun

In northern parts of the world the sun spends most of its time in the southern part of the sky. Trees, like all green plants, need the sun to thrive and so they reflect the sun's arc in the way they grow. The side that gets the most sun, the southern side in the UK, will grow more densely and appear 'heavier' than the side that's shaded by the trees' own leaves. This effect is easiest to spot in isolated deciduous trees, such as a big lone oak in a field.

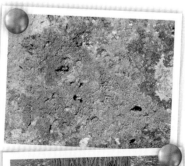

On stones, brown and orange coloured lichens can indicate the sunny south side, and moss the cooler north side. But again this can also be due to wind and the direction of water flow, so be careful.

## Man-made landscape

A church is a very useful indicator of direction if you know the basics of church alignment.

Traditionally, Christians build their churches with the chancel (the location of the altar, where the mass is celebrated) pointing eastwards, so that the congretation seated in the nave also faces eastwards. Therefore, the transepts that cross the nave are aligned north/south.

You'll rarely be far from a church as they are so numerous throughout the UK – the Church of England has over 16,000 churches in its care.

## The effect of wind

Trees and other natural features in the landscape are often indicators of the direction of the prevailing wind. The tree shown in the image below has been dramatically distorted by the force of the prevailing south-westerly wind (in the UK) which has also caused dehydration in the growth of new branches in the spring. The cumulative effect is that the tree acts almost like a signpost from the south-west to the north-east. Obvious soil erosion and the location of sand dunes can also be similar indicators.

# READING A LANDSCAPE

If two people go on exactly the same walk at the same time, one will have a richer experience than the other. It's up to us which of those walkers we choose to be.

## Look up

The sky makes up half of what we can see when we're outdoors, but we rarely give it the attention it deserves. Getting to know the sky's many characters enables us to notice so much that will pass others by – changing light levels, shifting colours, clouds that forecast the weather, the moon, stars, planets and even shadows in the sky at the start and end of the day. These ephemeral walking partners often appear and disappear while our concentration on texting and emails blots our senses.

## Look down

Search for patterns and shapes in the ground. There's an undiscovered world in the details of the ground we walk over. There are unusual shapes in the cracks of drying mud puddles and in the sand of beaches. Each patch of drying mud will form a unique pattern of cracks as it dries. As the waves retreat from a beach they form patterns, dimpled orange peel, chevrons like fish scales and whole trees. Each wave wipes these sculptures away and then forms new ones.

## Look around

Each time you see a hill or mountain, notice how the plants change as your eyes move from the bottom to the top. Each plant has conditions that suit it and this leads to bands of vegetation that change with altitude. Deciduous trees give way to conifers, which yield to hardier smaller plants like gorse and then grasses. And if it's high enough, eventually everything gives way to the snowline. The individual plants may change, but these bands can be found all over the world.

## Right to left

When reading a landscape, try moving your eyes from right to left and to use small skips. This is counterintuitive, as we normally read from left to right, so it acts as a brake. Small skips ensure that we use both direct and peripheral vision. Together these techniques can make us more observant.

## Stop & close your eyes

Our sense of sight is powerful – sometimes too powerful, as it bullies the other senses. So stop occasionally and close your eyes. Use your other senses to notice more, and to make new connections. You might smell the sea, which is north of you because there's a northerly breeze, which is also why you can feel a chill in the air. The irony is that stopping walking and closing our eyes can make a walk both more memorable and sensuous.

# GLOBAL POSITIONING SYSTEM (GPS)

GPS is becoming the preferred navigational tool for outdoor use; it's accurate, fast and, when there's signal, reliable. Just make sure that you have a basic knowledge of map and compass to fall back on.

## What is GPS?

GPS is an acronym that stands for Global Positioning System, a network of 24 satellites (plus spares) orbiting the Earth at approximately 12,000 miles. These satellites continuously transmit coded data via very low-power radio signals, making it possible for anyone with a GPS receiver to accurately determine locations on Earth by receiving signals from three or more satellites. The system is owned by the United States Military but became widely available for civilian use in May 2000. It can be used for free. A hand-held Global Positioning System receiver is usually referred to simply as a GPS.

The core function of a GPS is to tell you where you are. It allows you to record or create locations from places on Earth and helps you navigate to and from those spots. It can be used everywhere except where it's impossible to receive the signal. The signals travel 'line of sight', so they'll pass through clouds, glass and plastic, but won't go through solid objects such as mountains or buildings, subterranean locations or underwater.

GPS provides amazing accuracy. Basic survey units can offer accuracy down to 1m. More expensive systems can provide accuracy to within a centimetre.

## The three segments of GPS

### 1 Space segment (the satellites)

This is the heart of the system and consists of 24 satellites that orbit about 12,000 miles above the Earth's surface. They're arranged in their orbits so that a GPS receiver on Earth can always receive at least four of them at any given time.

### 2 Control segment (the ground stations)

This controls the GPS satellites by tracking them and providing them with corrected orbital and time information. There are five control stations located around the world.

### 3 User segment (you and your GPS receiver)

This is simply you and your GPS device, which might be a dedicated receiver, satnav, mobile phone, tablet or watch. In addition GPS technology may be found embedded in everything from cameras to combine harvesters.

## A look at the mechanics

Imagine circles drawn on a map. If you're 150 miles from London and 150 miles from Manchester, there are two possible places you can be. But if you also know your distance from Newcastle, you can work out which one you're at. A GPS uses this principle with the signal it gets from the satellites.

## GPS accuracy

The accuracy of GPS can be affected by several factors. If all the satellites whose signals are being received are in the same general direction, the triangulation will be poor because all the distance measurements are from the same direction. But four satellites at right angles will give excellent triangulation.

Buildings and trees can cause signal blockage or multi-pathing, much like ghost reception on an old-fashioned terrestrial TV channel. If the signal has bounced off a few buildings it will have taken longer to get to the receiver, thus your GPS will think the satellite is further away. Equally, atmospheric conditions can affect the signal as it travels through the ionosphere and troposphere.

## How does GPS work?

The GPS receiver needs to know two things: a) where the satellites are (location), and b) how far away they are (distance). The GPS picks up coded information from the satellites. Even though the GPS receiver knows the precise location of the satellites in space, it still needs to know how far away the satellites are so that it can determine its position on Earth. There's a simple formula that tells the receiver how far it is from each satellite (a bit like working out how far away a thunderstorm is by counting the seconds between seeing the lightning and hearing the thunder).

So once we have both satellite location and distance the receiver can determine a position. To determine your three-dimensional position (latitude, longitude and altitude), the receiver will lock on to four satellites. Once the GPS has calculated a position you're ready to start navigating. Most GPS units will display a position page or a page showing your position on a map (map screen) that will assist in your navigation.

The unit stores data about where the satellites are located at any given time. This data is called the almanac. Sometimes when the GPS unit isn't turned on for a length of time the almanac can get outdated, or 'cold'. When the GPS receiver is 'cold' it could take longer to acquire the satellites. A receiver is considered 'warm' when data has been collected from the satellites within the previous four to six hours.

Even with GPS technology becoming better every day, it's still a good idea to have back-up navigation. Having a map, compass and the knowledge to use them is good, safe and prudent practice. Remember, GPS is a complement to navigation and shouldn't be your only navigational tool.

# USING A GPS

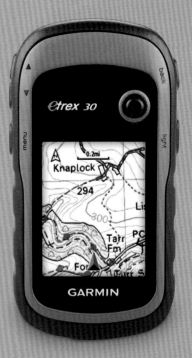

When used as a hand-held device for walking it's necessary to know which reference system is displayed, as there are many that either cover the entire globe or just a small area. It's also important to remember that a GPS is just another tool to navigation – it isn't a substitute for a map and compass. The signal may be lost or batteries may go flat.

A GPS will enable you to follow a bearing and know your location, even in fog. There are a wide variety of functions available on even the most basic of hand-held GPS devices. More advanced models will include electronic compass through to comprehensive maps, both inbuilt or on memory devices. Although all GPSs will give an indication of where north is, it's important to remember that a basic GPS has this information only while you're moving. This is because it's simply calculating your movements and where north is. If you change track, the GPS will take a few metres to detect the change and give you a different pointer to north. More advanced receivers will include an electronic compass and even a barometric altimeter.

There are clearly areas where a GPS can make your outdoor experience more interesting and safer. Even the most basic unit will enable waypoints to be entered to make up a route, so that it's possible to programme the GPS with the route plan for an entire hike, with the rest stops and direction changes plotted. It will display your average speed and tell you how long to the next waypoint or the end of the route. Any activity on open space, hills or at sea becomes much safer because a sudden fog will no longer stop you knowing where you are, where your destination is, and where you started from. Incident hikes, treasure hunts or any sort of journey can be enhanced by using GPS navigation.

# GEOCACHING WITH GPS

If you enjoy the outdoors and you have access to a GPS device then why not have a go at the high-tech treasure hunt known as geocaching? Anyone can take part, it costs nothing, and it can make any walk in the town or country that bit more interesting.

## What is geocaching?

It all started when an American wondered what would happen if he hid a container of trinkets and a logbook out in the wilderness and posted the coordinates on the internet. Would people go and look for it? They did, and now this activity – normally called geocaching – has grown into a recreational pursuit that covers the globe.

Geocaching involves participants seeking out hidden containers (caches) using the published coordinates. When found, they record the find in the log within the container and on the website that listed the location. Although other websites do exist, the activity is dominated by geocaching.com. Basic membership of the site is free, although advanced facilities are available for those willing to pay. Within the UK there are other websites that supplement the provisions of geocaching.com and provide essential information and rules specific to the UK.

## Geocaching and scouts

From a Scouting perspective it's important to remember that this activity is based on locating a hidden container, whilst simultaneously ensuring that non-geocachers don't find the cache. In many respects geocaching is very much in the spirit of Baden-Powell and *Scouting for Boys*: geocaching is an activity for the initiated, to be kept secret from those who might not be trusted to observe the code of conduct.

A geocache may be of any size from Micro (only large enough to hold a paper log and 35mm film canisters are frequently the receptacle of choice) to Regular (of several litres capacity). For the rural environment, a new cache category is appearing, the Nano, a specialist container large enough to hold no more than a long thin strip of paper, often magnetised and secured behind road signs or similar. Weather-sealing is an important consideration for all caches.

Geocaching.com specifies in their Cache Listing Requirements: 'Caches perceived to be posted for religious, political, charitable or social agendas are not permitted.' This doesn't prevent placing caches

that are owned by Scouts and that contain Scouting items. It's perfectly acceptable to state that a particular Scout Troop, Group or District own a cache and to give some Scouting information in the cache description, including a link to www.scouts.org.uk.Ultimately the information provided by the cache owner submitting the listing is reviewed by one of the moderators before release, but making a blatant recruitment advertisement from a cache listing would not be acceptable.

A search of geocaching.com for caches using the keyword 'scout' will reveal several hundred with a Scouting connection, principally in the USA, and often placed by Scouts. One notable cache is waypoint GCM40K at Paxtu, Baden-Powell's house in Kenya, and there are two in the grounds of Gilwell Park, the HQ of The Scout Association in the UK.

## Trading goodies

One of the guiding principles of geocaching is 'take something, leave something'. A geocache hider places a number of goodies in a container when a new cache is first started. As people find the cache, they exchange goodies that catch their eye with trade items they've brought with them on the search.

Common goodies include badges, key fobs, trading cards, whistles, bracelets, or indeed just about any low-value trinket you can think of. Sometimes the hider puts a real prize, say a £1 coin, in the cache at the start as a reward for the first person to find it.

Items of food, including sweets, should be avoided. Not only will foodstuffs deteriorate over time but if the container is not sealed completely then animals could be attracted – which is not always desirable.

# GEOCACHING TERMS

- **CITO** – Cache In Trash Out. A principle that should be followed by all cachers and that can result in specific CITO events. All cachers should do their bit to keep the countryside clean by collecting litter, but a CITO event is organised with that specific goal, being a community clean-up usually followed by a social gathering of geocachers with a cache hunt or two.

- **Geocache** – Often called simply a 'cache', the actual container placed at the waypoint. From 'geo', for Earth, and 'cache', a store of goods or supplies, often left by explorers.

- **Geocaching** – A recreational activity that entails seeking a container hidden at specific coordinates: finding it, recording your details on the log within, then concealing it for the next person.

- **Multi-cache** – A type of cache that requires several waypoints to complete. The first waypoint may contain a small cache containing the coordinates of the next stage, or several waypoints might each contain components of the coordinates for the final waypoint.

- **Trackback** – The ability to reverse a route on a GPS to enable the user to return to their starting point.

- **Track log** – The ability of the GPS to automatically record track points; an electronic 'breadcrumb trail'.

- **Travel bug** – An item with an identity tag attached, which through a unique tracking number can be followed on the internet as it's moved from cache to cache by geocachers.

- **WAAS** – Wide Area Augmentation System. A Federal Aviation Administration-funded project to improve GPS accuracy in North America. There is the potential for a similar system in Europe, as the EU is planning to set up its own GPS service.

- **Waypoint** – A specific point defined by coordinates, which may be programmed into a GPS in advance or marked along a route whilst at the location, for example to return to the same point later.

# TRACKING IN THE WILD

Every living creature leaves a trace behind; learning to interpret these clues is the first step to take in the art of tracking. Another word for tracking, of course, is Scouting.

## Tracking origins

We've been tracking ever since, and probably before, we evolved into Homo Sapiens. It was fundamental to our search for food and hence our survival. As our brains evolved we started to improve our interpretation of the signs that animals left behind, which eventually led us to more ingenious ways of following, finding and catching our quarry.

Hundreds of thousands of years later, the principles of tracking remain the same. Every living creature will leave a mark or sign of its presence upon the earth. All we have to do, as trackers, is find these marks, interpret them and, perhaps, successfully follow them.

But it's not just about the footprints in the sand. It's also about other signs that animals leave behind – a dislodged stone, a feeding sign, some droppings, a broken twig, or a hair caught on barbed wire. Once we put these together a story unfolds, and we can build a picture of what happened, even though we weren't there to see it.

On our journey we must learn about our own surroundings: the woods and the environment and, of course, the creatures in it. We must also learn to use and enhance what skills we have to pit our wits against our quarry.

Baden-Powell himself sought the expertise of trackers, and he utilised native people's ability to observe, track and remain undetected. They were called Scouts.

At its most basic the ancient art and science of tracking is easy to learn, but takes a lifetime to master. Of course, it doesn't have to be an animal you're looking for. Tracking can involve searching for people, which may include people who are lost or missing.

Tracking crosses the borders between age, gender, culture and even disability. It teaches patience. It hones deductive skills. It opens your senses. It makes you look at how nature interacts with itself and us. It gets you outdoors. It builds a team. It gets you closer to the environment. It teaches you about yourself. But there's much, much more.

Most of us can already track. We've just forgotten how.

## Signs of otters

The otter is one of our most charismatic semi-aquatic mammals. When not diving in seas and rivers for prey such as fish, frogs and crabs, otters spend a good deal of their time simply playing. Get to know their distinctive pawprints and droppings and you will soon track one down.

# BADEN-POWELL ON TRACKING

Robert Baden-Powell, the founder of Scouting, was a legendary tracker during his military days in South Africa and Afghanistan. He passed on his thoughts on the subject in his many books, notably *Scouting for Boys*.

Such was Baden-Powell's skill in making himself invisible – through sensitivity to his environment, patience and powers of observation – that his men gave him the nickname The Wolf That Never Sleeps.

'Observation and deduction are the basis of all knowledge,' he wrote. 'The importance of the power of observation and deduction to the young citizen can therefore not be underestimated. Observation is in fact a habit in which you have to be trained. Tracking is an interesting step towards gaining it. Deduction is the art of subsequently reasoning out and extracting the meaning from the points observed.

'When you want to observe wild animals, you have to stalk them, that is, creep up on them without their seeing or smelling you. Carry out two important things when you don't want to be seen.

'Firstly, take care that the ground behind you, or trees, or building, is the same colour as your clothes. The other is if the animal is seen looking for you, remain perfectly still without moving so long as he is there. In choosing your background, consider the colour of your clothes; thus, if you are dressed in khaki, don't go and stand in front of a white-washed wall, or in front of a dark-shaded bush, but go where there is khaki-coloured sand or grass or rocks behind you – and remain perfectly still.

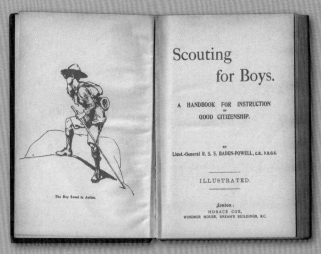

'If you are in dark clothes, get among dark bushes, or in the shadow of trees or rocks, but be careful that the ground beyond you is also dark – if there is a light-coloured ground beyond the trees under which you are standing, for instance, you will stand out clearly defined against it.

'In making use of hills as lookout places, be very careful not to show yourself on the top or skyline. Crawl on all fours, lying flat in the grass; on reaching the top, very slowly raise your head, inch by inch until you can see the view. If you think you are being watched, keep your head perfectly steady for an extended period of time and you should be mistaken for a lump or stone. Afterwards, gradually lower your head, inch by inch into the grass again and crawl quietly away. Any quick or sudden movement of the head on the skyline would be liable to attract attention, even at a considerable distance.

'To keep hidden while moving, especially at night, walk quietly. The thump of an ordinary person's heel on the ground can be heard a good distance off, but a Scout walks lightly on the ball of his boot, not his heel, and thus you should practise whenever you are walking by day or by night, indoors as well as out, so that it becomes a habit.

'When stalking a wild animal, you must keep downwind of it even if the wind is so slight as to be merely a slight air. Be sure which way the wind is blowing and work up against it. To find this out, you should wet your thumb and hold it up to see which side is coldest, or you can throw some light dust, or dry grass or leaves in the air, and see which way they drift.'

# TRACKING SIGNS

Tracking is one of the great Scouting skills. Like other animals, we also leave prints, but we can be far more sophisticated in the signs or symbols we deliberately leave behind. These are usually made from natural materials on a trail or course, for others to follow.

### Direction
This is the basic directional arrow – it can be made from sticks, stones or even twisted grass.

### Turn left or right
A variation on the basic directional symbol, this could just as easily be a sheaf of grass twisted or bent over.

### Not this way
Try and anticipate where people may go wrong (at the fork in a road for example) and use this symbol.

### Over obstacle
Sometimes a trail can be lost if it has to cross a fence or stream; use a symbol like this to keep people on track.

### Water in this direction
This could have life-saving consequences one day if used in a real emergency situation.

### Message this way
A more unusual symbol, indicating a note is close by – perhaps left in the branches of a tree or on a rock?

### Party split up
This simply indicates that the main party has split and is now following two separate paths.

### Gone home
This indicates the end of the trail; it's back to base. Also used in place of RIP in Scouting.

### Sticks and stones
Tracking can provide the basis for various kinds of outdoor games, and trails are easy to set up – all you need is a supply of sticks or stones. Choose a wooded area with various features (fallen trees, hedges, twists and turns), and always agree on an 'end of activity' signal beforehand, to call people back to the start of a trail. A long blast on a whistle is ideal for this.

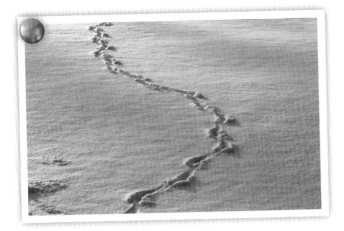

## The tracking stick

Tracking is such a primitive skill that it can be considered the first-ever science. This belief is taken up in modern forensic science, where one of the main principles is that 'every contact leaves a trace'. In other words, if there's contact between two surfaces, there will be evidence of that contact – however minute. Unfortunately, most trackers don't have access to advanced scientific equipment. We have to rely on our primary senses, mainly that of sight. But if we look at the principle a little closer we can use something to help us predict where the next footprint may be – even though initially we might not even see it. This is the tracking stick.

The principle of the tracking stick has its roots in man-tracking. US border agent Jack Kearney developed the simple technique of using a straight stick with a couple of rubber bands to measure the known stride-length of his quarry. Taking the principle of 'every contact leaves a trace', the next footprint should be within an arc made by the tip of the tracking stick at a similar length of the known stride.

## Prehistoric tracking

Similar techniques were used by paleontologists when tracking dinosaurs; piecing together their hunting and breeding behaviour was only possible by studying and measuring their fossilised remains. Same methods; bigger feet!

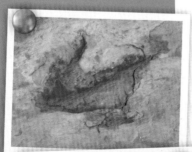

## How to make a tracking stick

Tracking sticks are great fun and easy to make. Many trackers add feathers or small compasses and carve paw prints or even faces into their sticks. Their sticks are treasured items, as well as being practical. Try to make one yourself.

**1** Select a straight piece of wood that comes up to your waist. Don't select wood that's too heavy or too thick – it isn't a walking stick. Coppiced hazel is good.

**2** Sharpen one end to a point and cut the other end straight.

**3** Get at least three small rubber bands. Attach these tightly to the stick to form a ring (it doesn't matter where yet). They will be used to measure the stride of various animals.

**4** Customise your stick to suit your personal tastes – add feathers, for instance, or carve animal prints into it.

## How to use a tracking stick

A tracking stick is used mainly to measure a stride – it gives a reasonably precise measure of where to look for the next print.

**1** Measure your quarry's known stride from heel to toe by moving the rubber band (red mark).

**2** Putting the rubber band mark on the toe of the print, swing the stick in an arc and look for any marks in the soil caused by the heel of the next footprint.

**3** You can use a second rubber band to measure the foot or shoe size. This will give you a completely new track.

**4** Additional rubber bands could measure the straddle or pitch of your quarry. An experienced tracker can tell many things from changes in straddle and pitch, such as if the quarry is getting tired.

# ANIMAL TRACKS

All animals leave telltale signs behind them for any keen wildlife detective to observe, from droppings to evidence of a half-eaten lunch, but it's their tracks that provide the most accurate means of identification.

## Small mammals

These are telltale tracks of smaller mammals which frequent our gardens, woods and forests.

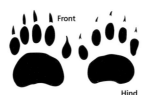
**Badger**

**Red Fox**

**Domestic dog**

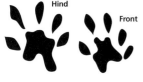
**Otter**

**Mink**

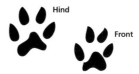
**Weasel**

**Domestic cat**

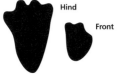
**Hare**

**Rabbit**

**Squirrel**

**Hedgehog**

**Mouse**

## Injured animals

If you spend a good deal of time outdoors it's inevitable that at some point you'll come across an injured animal or bird. It may have been injured by another animal, in a fight with its own species or perhaps as a result of human activity. The advice for dealing with them is similar to helping a human casualty. Stay as calm as possible yourself, which will also reassure the animal. As it may need to undergo emergency surgery, don't give it food or water; just try and keep it still and warm. Call the RSPCA 24-hour cruelty and advice line on 0300 1234 999. They'll ask for a description of the animal's injuries and your location, and will offer advice and may even attend.

## Hoofed animals

These are the shapes to learn if you're looking for evidence of larger mammals in a particular area.

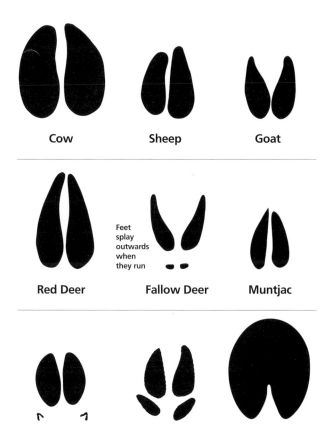

Cow     Sheep     Goat

Red Deer     Fallow Deer     Muntjac

Feet splay outwards when they run

Wild Boar     Pig     Horse

## Birds

You will need to look closer for the finer imprints left by birds, although their tracks are equally distinctive.

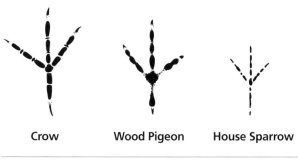

Crow     Wood Pigeon     House Sparrow

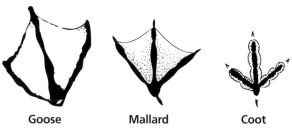

Goose     Mallard     Coot

# WILDLIFE PHOTOGRAPHY

Our advice for taking the best wildlife pictures that you can.

**1 Get up early**
You often see the best wildlife at dawn. The light at this time of day can also be highly atmospheric.

**2 Choose a good camera**
This should be a good digital SLR camera; you may also need telephoto lenses for long-range work or macro lenses for close-up work.

**3 Get up close**
But keep yourself out of sight; hide behind natural objects or even your car to avoid scaring your subject. Remember to stay downwind of your subject to avoid detection.

**4 Go steady**
Use a tripod if you can. No matter how steady your hand, the results will be better with some sturdy mechanical support.

**5 Practice**
Your garden is as good a place as the Scottish Highlands to take some amazing photographs.

**6 Study behaviour**
Getting to know your subject is a must; find out its habitat, food, likes and dislikes.

**7 Go for active shots**
Wildlife interacting, feeding or in flight makes for a more compelling shot than a static portrait.

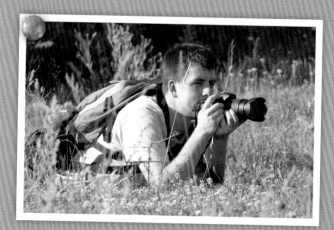

# COMMUNICATION
## AND SIGNALS

Good communication is vitally important when exploring in remote areas and never more so than when you need help or rescue. Not only do you need a reliable way to make contact with the outside world, you also need a reliable contingency you can depend on.

## Signal fires

Signal fires have been used for centuries as a method of conveying information over large distances – soldiers in Ancient China, native North Americans and the ancient Greeks all had their own methods of sending and receiving messages in this way. Fire is also a very effective means of getting help – its smoke can be seen by day, and its flames stand out at night. Always ensure your fire is well away from nearby trees and bushes, to prevent setting them alight.

## Smoke signals

It's very simple to send and receive smoke signals. All you need to do before you start is agree a code between sender and receiver: one puff means an 'enemy' is approaching, two means they've been captured, for example – use your imagination! You may even find it possible to use Morse code to send more complex messages.

As everyone knows, there's no smoke without fire, so your first priority is to build one. Do it in an open area as high up as you can (see page 134 onwards for hints and tips on firelighting). It goes without saying that you must take every precaution to ensure you don't accidentally ignite the surrounding vegetation. Adhere to the campfire safety checklist that you will find set out on page 149.

Once you have the fire going well, add grass and green

sticks and branches – these will smother the flames and create a dense, white smoke. You'll need to make sure you also have a good supply of wood ready to burn, as grass and green sticks won't fuel your fire for long.

When you're ready to send your message, soak an old blanket in water (to keep it from burning) and carefully throw it over the smoking fire. This will stop the trail of smoke. When you're ready, pull the blanket off to send a white puff up to the sky; then put the blanket back on. This will send a one-puff message.

Once you've finished sending and receiving your smoke signals, don't forget to make sure your fire is fully extinguished, and that you've left the area tidy and as you found it.

# MORSE CODE

Morse code is a method of sending messages using lights or tones, where each character or number is represented by short or long signals – dots or dashes.

|  |  |
|--------|------|
| A | · — |
| B | — · · · |
| C | — · — · |
| D | — · · |
| E | · |
| F | · · — · |
| G | — — · |
| H | · · · · |
| I | · · |
| J | · — — — |
| K | — · — |
| L | · — · · |
| M | — — |
| N | — · |
| O | — — — |
| P | · — — · |
| Q | — — · — |
| R | · — · |

|  |  |
|---------------|------|
| S | · · · |
| T | — |
| U | · · — |
| V | · · · — |
| W | · — — |
| X | — · · — |
| Y | — · — — |
| Z | — — · · |
| 1 | · — — — — |
| 2 | · · — — — |
| 3 | · · · — — |
| 4 | · · · · — |
| 5 | · · · · · |
| 6 | — · · · · |
| 7 | — — · · · |
| 8 | — — — · · |
| 9 | — — — — · |
| 0 | — — — — — |

|  | |  |
|--------|--|------|
| Full stop | . | · — · — · — |
| Comma | , | — — · · — — |
| Question mark | ? | · · — — · · |
| Apostrophe | ' | · — — — — · |
| Exclamation mark | ! | — · — · — — |
| Slash, fraction bar | / | — · · — · |
| Open brackets | ( | — · — — · |
| Close brackets | ) | — · — — · — |
| Ampersand, wait | & | · — · · · |
| Colon | : | — — — · · · |
| Semicolon | ; | — · — · — · |
| Double dash | = | — · · · — |
| Plus | + | · — · — · |
| Hyphen, minus | - | — · · · · — |
| Underscore | _ | · · — — · — |
| Quotation mark | " | · — · · — · |
| Dollar sign | $ | · · · — · · — |
| At sign | @ | · — — · — · |

## Dot, dot, dash

The duration of a dash is three times the duration of a dot. Each dot or dash is followed by a short silence, equal to the dot duration. The letters of a word are separated by a space equal to three dots (one dash), and two words are separated by a space equal to seven dots.

Morse code has traditionally been used by amateur radio users, in aviation and at sea, but is also widely used in the outdoors, especially in emergencies. The international distress call 'SOS' is probably the most famous, and easy to learn – dot-dot-dot-dash-dash-dash-dot-dot-dot.

Signals can be sent visually (for example by flashes from a torch) or audibly (for example by using a specialist 'key', but an air horn or whistle would work just as well).

# SEMAPHORE

Semaphore is a long-established system of signalling using hand-held flags. It's a great way of conveying messages over a distance where the sender and receiver can see each other. The flags are held, with arms extended, in various positions that represent each of the letters of the alphabet.

## Ground-to-air signals

Although it's to be hoped you'll never need them, there's a recognised series of symbols for communication with emergency air crews. It's well worth familiarising yourself with this before walking or climbing in remote areas.

Make the markers as large as possible. The recommended size for each symbol is 3m wide by 10m long, with about 3m between symbols if you need to use more than one. Use rocks or logs, or make grooves in the ground. Better still, use your backpacks, groundsheets or anything else that will stand out.

## Aircraft response

If your message is spotted and understood, the pilot will waggle the aircraft's wings in a rocking motion, or if at night will flash green lights on and off. If the pilot cannot understand your message, the plane will fly clockwise in a right-handed circle in daylight, or flash red lights on and off at night.

 We have an injury and need a doctor

 I am unable to move

 Affirmative / Yes ('Y' is also understood as 'Yes')

 All is well

 I need medical supplies

 I am moving this way

 Negative / No

 I do not understand

 I need food and water

 I need a compass and a map

 Please indicate in which direction I should travel

 I think it is safe to land here

## Body signals

**Pick us up**

**Need mechanical help**

**All is well**

**No**

**Yes**

**Can proceed shortly**

**Have radio**

**Land here**

**Do not attempt to land**

**Use drop message**

**Need medical assistance**

## Moving on

If you decide to or have to move on, remember to leave a clear indication of your direction of travel, frequent written and dated messages (leave these in visible elevated positions, such as in trees), and further tracking symbols so that rescuers can follow your route.

# TOOLS AND GADGETS

You only need to walk into an outdoors shop or spend a minute online to see the huge variety of outdoors equipment available. Tents with inflatable poles, apps that recognise mountain ranges, remote-control LED lights and the infamous 'spork' (a combined spoon and fork)... there's a mind-boggling array of gadgetry on sale. In reality, however, very little of this gear is actually needed. Apart from a few basic items such as an axe, saw and knives, all you really require is a healthy dose of commonsense and a willingness to learn. Besides, it's much more fun and certainly cheaper if you learn how to make some of these gadgets for yourself.

# USING AN AXE

Axes have been used for thousands of years to split and cut wood. Largely unchanged in shape, the modern axe needs to be handled with care and skill to ensure both safety and efficient use. Handling an axe is a skill that once learned is rarely forgotten.

## Types of axe

There are two main kinds of axe: the hand axe and the felling axe. Both have either a wooden or metal handle, the latter variety being a one-piece construction in which the blade and handle are a single unit. Hand axes are for use on smaller pieces of wood (no more than about 10cm across), whereas a felling axe is for larger trunks and for cutting down trees.

Axes should always be stored safely, preferably with a mask over the blade to protect both it and you. The blade should be kept sharp by using a sharpening stone and should be greased to prevent it from rusting.

To carry any axe, hold the head in your hand with the blade pointing forwards, the handle pointing skywards, and your arm straight down by your side.

## Chopping wood

To chop a piece of wood with an axe you should:

**1** Place the wood on a chopping block (a substantial log or similar). Kneel or stand behind the block.

**2** Hold the wood to be chopped in one hand and the axe by the handle in the other.

**3** Chop the wood by keeping the axe and the lower part of your arm straight, bending your arm at the shoulder.

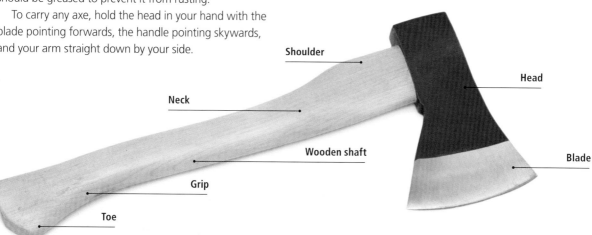

Shoulder

Head

Neck

Wooden shaft

Blade

Grip

Toe

## Using a felling axe

A felling axe is a powerful tool that can help you do a large amount of work in a short space of time. To avoid injury or over-exertion, it's important to understand the technique that allows the tool to work as hard as you. As the axe head cuts across the grain of the wood, the axe blade should be kept as sharp as possible.

**1** Place the wood on a flat piece of ground so that it cannot move. Stand facing the wood so that it lies from left to right in front of you.

**2** Place your feet slightly apart so that if you should miss, the axe will pass between them. The blade should rest on the wood and the handle should be in your hand without you having to lean forward.

**3** With both hands on the handle, place one at the top by the head and the other at the toe, with the axe upright in front of you.

**4** Then let the head fall and as it does so your hand at the top will slide down the handle to the foot. The weight of the head should do the work and you shouldn't need to 'force' it down. Make a V shape when cutting as before.

**5** When cutting an upright tree follow the procedures above, but this time you'll swing the axe horizontally.

# SAFETY CHECK
# USING AN AXE

Each axe should only be used for the purpose for which it was designed. It should be properly cared for and only handled by those who know how to use it.

- Any defective parts should be replaced or mended before use. Axes should be sharpened using the proper sharpening stone and lubricant. This should be a round carborundum stone, which is available in different grades of coarseness. You should start with a coarse one initially and finish with a fine grade. Oil is the lubricant that should be used with a sharpening stone.

- You should ensure that you have the correct clothing for working with axes. Make sure that all loose clothing is secured to avoid it being caught or getting in the way. A good pair of thick gardening gloves will protect your hands from minor nicks and abrasions. Strong shoes or boots (ideally with hardened toecaps) will protect your feet if an axe slips or any wood you're cutting falls on your feet. You might also consider the use of safety glasses or goggles, which can prevent wood clippings from getting in your eyes.

- Before using an axe ensure that other people are aware of what you're doing and that you have a clear area around you, free from people and obstacles – about three times the length of the handle is a rough rule of thumb. Also ensure that there's nothing overhead that your axe could get snagged on.

- Using an axe gets tiring after a while so always stop and rest periodically. A sure sign you're getting tired is when you're no longer accurately directing the axe head to make the V shape. If you're with someone else who's competent in using the axe, let them have a go for a while until they get tired and hand back to you.

- Always make sure that the blade of your axe is covered when transporting it or putting it away after use. Either use a plastic 'clip-on' mask or tie a length of sacking around the blade.

# USING A SAW

Along with the axe, the saw is the backwoodsman's indispensable tool for cutting and shaping wood. Which type you use, however, depends on the kind of wood you're cutting as well as the speed and accuracy required.

## Types of saw

The most common hand saw is called a cross-cut saw, used to cut across the grain of the wood. A rip saw has bigger teeth and can cut with the grain. For making curves or circles, a coping saw is used (shaped like the letter D) although the depth of the cut will be restricted by the design of the saw. Back saws are fitted with a metal bracing and are ideal when you need to make a more accurate cut. The bow saw is used frequently in the outdoors; it has large teeth and will cut quickly, although imprecisely through a log or branch.

## Using a wire saw

In an outdoor setting, a wire saw is generally used for cutting logs for firewood. It takes up much less space in your kit than a hand saw and is also reasonably accurate. However, without a handle, the leverage is reduced and it takes longer to make your cut. The wire is also more liable to break than the blade of a conventional saw.

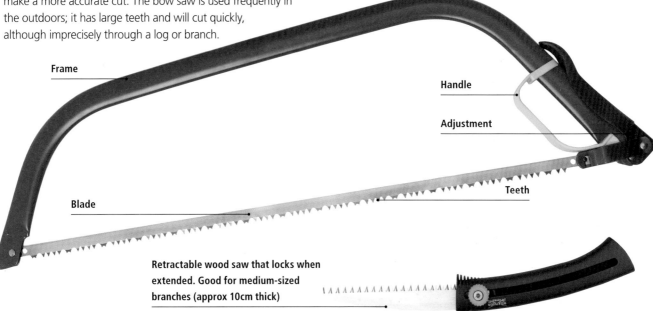

Frame

Handle

Adjustment

Teeth

Blade

Retractable wood saw that locks when extended. Good for medium-sized branches (approx 10cm thick)

## Sawing wood

The typical saw that's used for cutting wood outdoors is the bow saw or a variation called a bush saw. Essentially the use and care of both types is very similar and the same instructions apply for each.

A saw is a safer and easier tool to use than an axe, particularly for the novice who hasn't cut wood before. To use a bow saw you should:

**1** Make sure that the wood is held firmly – if you need to use your hand for this, keep it well away from the blade and preferably wear a thick gardening-type glove.

**2** Start slowly – pull the blade backwards towards you until it has cut a groove into the wood. You may need to repeat this backwards action several times before you're able to saw using a forward motion.

**3** Push and pull in a steady rhythm, using the whole length of the blade.

**4** Ensure that the gaps between the teeth on the blade don't get clogged with sawdust – this is particularly likely with wood that hasn't fully dried out and is still 'green'.

**5** Be aware as you cut that if the wood is touching the ground the cut will close and trap the blade. If possible, therefore, try to keep the end of the wood off the ground so that the cut will open as you saw, allowing the blade to work effectively.

**6** If needed, cut a V in the wood to prevent the blade being pinched as the weight of the wood squeezes the cut.

# SAFETY CHECK
# USING A SAW

Every tool should only be used for the purpose for which it was designed. It should be properly cared for and only handled by those who know how to use it.

- Any defective parts should be replaced or mended before use. As saw blades are relatively cheap it's advisable to replace them rather than to attempt to sharpen them.

- You should ensure that you have the correct clothing for working with a saw. Make sure that all loose clothing is secured to avoid it being caught in a saw or getting in the way. Thick gloves will protect your hands from minor nicks and abrasions. Strong shoes or boots (ideally with hardened toecaps) will protect your feet if any wood you're cutting falls on them. You might also consider the use of safety glasses or goggles, which can prevent sawdust from getting in your eyes.

- Before using a saw ensure that other people are aware of what you're doing and that you have a clear area around you, free from people and obstacles.

- Using a saw gets tiring after a while so always stop and rest periodically. A sure sign you're getting tired is when the saw blade keeps 'jumping' or sticking. If you're with someone else who's competent in using the tool, let them have a go for a while until they get tired and hand back to you.

- Always make sure that the blade of your saw is covered when transporting it or putting it away after use. Either use a plastic 'clip-on' mask or tie a length of sacking around the blade.

# USING A KNIFE

The knife is the key item of kit for the great outdoors – essential for firelighting, rope work and preparing food. However, it must be treated with great respect and only used after proper training.

## Safety first

Knives should be considered as tools and treated as such. Those who are going to use them should receive training in their use, as they would for a saw or an axe. Knives are dangerous, so great care should be taken when dealing with them. When undertaking training, knives should be taken to and from Scout meetings by an adult. When taking a knife to camp it should be securely stowed in the middle of the rucksack or bag.

The main UK legislation regarding the possession of knives and other sharply pointed/bladed objects is the Criminal Justice Act 1988. This details what's generally deemed to be an 'offensive' weapon, and Section 139 in particular describes the types of knives that are banned and those that can be carried in public (and under what circumstances).

## Types of knife

If you consider a knife as a tool then you should choose the appropriate tool for the job. The vast majority of Scout usage requires only a pen or clasp knife for cutting string, cooking or whittling. This should be a folding knife with a cutting blade no longer than three inches (7.62cm). Where you have a bigger task, such as splitting wood, a larger knife such as a sheath knife may be appropriate.

Here is a list of various knives and their uses:
- **Bread knife** This has a serrated blade with a blunt end
- **Dive knife** This has a plastic handle and hardened sheaf
- **Filet knife** For working with fish, meat and chicken
- **Utility knife** Mainly for carpentry purposes, with storage for spare blades
- **Scalpel** Generally for medical use only

Serrated edge – good for cutting rope

Good solid blade that doesn't corrode easily

Protective scabbard that covers the blade when housed

Well-constructed body that locks the blade in position

Well-shaped and constructed handle that grips well and is non-slip

## Multitools

Multitools, most based on the famous Leatherman variety, have become essential to those working outdoors. Incorporating a good-quality folding knife, they also contain tools as diverse as a saw, tape measure, screwdriver, pliers and corkscrew.

### Basic use

Always cut away from yourself; the most efficient method is to hold the piece of wood out to your side at about waist height then cut out and down, letting your shoulder rather than your arm do the hard work.

You can also hold the knife in a reverse grip (so the blade is pointing towards your knuckles) just above waist height. Holding the piece of wood in your other hand, cut outwards.

For additional support, strength and direction, you can also place your thumb on the back of the blade. This will give you more control when carving and making your cut.

# SAFETY CHECK
# USING A KNIFE

Every tool should only be used for the purpose for which it was designed. It should be properly cared for and only handled by those who know how to use it.

- A knife should only be carried when you know there's a job it'll be needed for – after all, you wouldn't carry an axe around a campsite on the off chance of coming across some wood to chop! Consequently knives should always be stowed away until such time as they're needed. As we've already said, legally you're not allowed to carry a knife in a public place without lawful authority or a reasonable excuse anyway, and although a campsite may technically be private property, even if owned by a District or County, it's considered as public property because of its use.

- If you're using a knife while sitting down, ensure that your chair, log or stone is stable; it mustn't wobble or rock. You should anchor your elbows on your knees and cut away from you. This keeps the blade well away from the legs and torso.

- If you're careful, a knife can be used for splitting wood. Place the knife at a right angle to the top of a long, thin piece of wood with the length of the blade pointing downwards towards the top of the wood. Ensure that your blade is longer than the diameter of the wood you're splitting – in other words that there's enough of the knife sticking out at the end. Using a large piece of wood and without holding the wood, firmly strike the end of the knife – this should result in a clean lengthways split.

- The safety precautions when using a knife should be no less strict that when you are using an axe or saw. Ensure that you work within a clearly defined area; that people are aware of what you are doing; that you are clear from any branches or undergrowth; and that there is no one you could accidentally strike with the knife if it were to slip from your hand. Always return the knife to its sheath, holder or folded position after use.

# KNIFE SHARPENING

Consistent sharpening doesn't require expensive or complicated equipment. All you need is a combination oilstone and an old leather belt. Find a flat surface that won't be damaged by oil. If you're outdoors a chopping block is ideal. Place the stone with its coarse side up. Apply plenty of oil.

**1** Start with the knife on the end of the stone nearest to you. With the cutting edge facing away from you, tilt the knife until you achieve the correct bevel angle. Move the knife away from you along the stone, applying pressure with your fingers towards the leading edge of the knife.

**2** Draw the knife across the stone as you move it forwards, so that you cover the entire length of the knife. As the blade curves up towards the tip the bevel loses contact with the stone. To compensate, slightly lift the handle towards the end of the sharpening stroke. That way the curved tip of the knife dips, and remains in contact with the sharpening stone.

**3** Where metal has been removed from the bevel, it will show as obvious scratches or shiny areas. If your technique is correct you'll see that metal has been removed from the whole bevel. If not, adjust the angles as necessary.

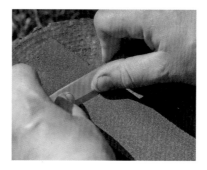

**4** To sharpen the opposite bevel, turn the cutting edge to face you and place the knife on the furthest end of the sharpening stone.

**5** Draw the knife along the stone towards you. Use your thumbs to apply pressure.

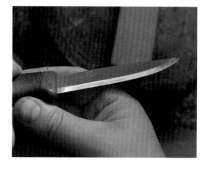

**6** As you take metal off each bevel you create a very thin foil where the bevels meet. Sometimes referred to as a burr, this is pushed one way then the other as you alternate your sharpening strokes.

## Achieving the correct bevel

You must remove metal from both bevels of a knife in order to form a fine edge where they meet. To achieve the correct bevel angle, place your knife flat on the stone then tilt the knife towards the cutting edge until the bevel is flush with the stone.

## Sharpening system

To ensure you're removing metal equally from both bevels you need a system to track the number of sharpening strokes you apply to each side of the knife. The method should also take the knife to a progressively finer edge.

1. Start with the coarse side of the stone up and apply oil.
2. Make eight strokes away from you.
3. Turn the knife and make eight strokes towards you.
4. Repeat steps 2 and 3 until the edge starts to feel like it has a burr.
5. Make one stroke away from you.
6. Make one stroke towards you.
7. Repeat steps 5 and 6 (ie alternating one stroke away then one towards) 10–20 times.
8. Swap to the finer side of the stone and apply oil.
9. Repeat steps 2 and 3 (ie eight strokes one way then eight the other) three or four times.
10. Repeat steps 5 and 6, 10–20 times.

## To finish off: stropping

To smooth the edge and remove any remaining burr, strop your knife on a tough leather belt.

Attach the belt to a solid upright. Grip your knife in one hand and the belt in the other. Run the blade along the unfinished (reverse) of the belt, leading with the back of the knife (with the sharp edge trailing).

The angle should be above the angle of the bevel so that you're slightly scraping the belt with the edge of the knife. Draw the blade across the strop as you move along it, so as to cover the whole length of the blade. Alternate the stropping strokes back and forth; 50–100 strokes are usually enough. Your knife should now be razor-sharp.

# KNIVES AND THE LAW

As someone who is likely to use a knife in the outdoors, or as someone responsible for others who will, it is essential that you familiarise yourself with the legal framework.

## Buying/selling knives

It's illegal for any shop to sell a knife of any kind (including cutlery, kitchen knives or Swiss Army knives) to anyone under the age of 18 (in England, Northern Ireland and Wales) or under the age of 16 (Scotland).

## Carrying knives

In general, it's an offence to carry a knife in a public place without good reason or lawful authority (for example, a good reason is a chef on his way to work and carrying his own knives). However, it isn't illegal to carry a foldable, non-locking knife – like a Swiss Army knife – in a public place so long as the blade is shorter than three inches (7.62cm).

There's an issue with regard to clasp knives and lock knives. A lock knife is one where the blade stays open unless some mechanism is used to close it. In the eyes of the Law, this multiple action makes it more of an offensive weapon than a standard clasp knife. From a safety point of view, however, a lock knife cannot fold on to the user's fingers and may be better.

## Maximum penalty

It is simply not worth running the risk of being caught with a knife that exceeds the stated limit. The police are unlikely to accept your explanation that you are 'simply using the knife in the outdoors'. An adult caught carrying an illegal knife in public currently faces a maximum fine of £5,000 and four years in prison.

For more information go to:
www.direct.gov.uk
and click on 'Crime Prevention'.

# PROJECT:
# CARVING A SPOON

To carve a simple spoon you'll need an axe, a knife, a hook knife of your choice and a log approximately 7cm in diameter and 30cm long.

**Difficulty**       **Total time** Allow 3 hours

**1** Split the log down the middle, and slightly offset the split to remove the heartwood.

**2** Take off the bark.

**3** Clean up the wood and chop a stop cut both sides at the bowl end. Chop the stop cut and remove the waste down one side of the handle.

**4** Do the same on the other side and you have the simple spoon shape.

**5** You can leave the spoon handle straight if you choose, but here we will make it curved.

**8** ...and shape the front underside.

**11** Carve the transition under the bowl and gently remove any rough work by holding the blade at 90° to the wood and using a scraping action along the grain.

**6** Carve from one end into the middle, then turn the spoon and carve from the other end into the middle.

**9** Carve the rounded bowl shape and tidy up all the other work with a good sharp knife.

**12** Your finished spoon will look something like this.

**7** The next step is to chop a flat-sided hollow into the bowl...

**10** The next job is to carve out the bowl. Carve across the grain to start with, then carve with the grain from one end of the bowl to the middle; turn the spoon and do the same from the other end.

**13** Let the spoon dry a while and then give it a thin coat of oil of your choice.

# KNOTS AND LASHINGS

Whether you're climbing, pioneering or angling, knots and lashings form an essential part of your outdoor knowledge. Practise in your spare time and you'll soon know the difference between a bend and a bight .

## Knots

People have been tying knots for thousands of years, and despite modern technology they remain as vital as ever today. In sports such as sailing, climbing, caving and angling, and in work such as firefighting, fishing, truck driving and even surgery, the ability to tie the right knot is essential.

All knots have a purpose, and it's just as important to understand what that purpose is, and when the knot should be used, as it is to be able to tie it. Using the wrong knot at the wrong time can be dangerous.

## How ropes are measured

Ropes are normally measured by their circumference. For example, a 75mm rope is approximately 25mm in diameter.

## Hanking a rope

Hanking your rope prevents it from getting knotted while in storage. Wrap the rope around your thumb and little finger in a figure of eight. Now, holding the roped bundle together, remove with your other hand and wind the free length firstly over itself, and then back down the length. Pull the short free end to find the loop that draws in. Form a loop with the standing end through, pulling it firmly. The hank should now be tight. To free the whole rope, pull on both ends.

## Rope terminology

You won't need to be told that a piece of rope has two ends! However, in order to work with ropes it's useful to understand the terminology used to describe their different parts.

- **Working end**
  The end of the rope you're using to tie a knot.

- **Standing part** Any part between the two ends.

- **Standing end**
  The opposite end of a rope to that being used to tie the knot.

- **Loop** A loop made by turning the rope back on itself and crossing the standing part.

- **Bight** A loop made by turning the rope back on itself without crossing the standing part.

- **Bend** A knot used for tying one rope to another.

- **Hitch** A means of fastening a rope to another object – such as a post, spar, pole or log – without using a full knot.

## Types of rope

### Laid ropes

These normally consist of three strands that run over each other from left to right. Traditionally they're made from natural fibres. Nowadays they tend more often to be made from synthetic materials.

### Braided ropes

These consist of a strong core of synthetic fibres, covered by a plaited or braided sheath. They're always made from synthetic materials.

### Natural ropes

These are relatively cheap and are made from such natural materials as hemp, sisal, manila and cotton. Their main disadvantage is in having a relatively low breaking point.

### Synthetic ropes

These are relatively expensive but last a long time. They're superior to natural ropes in that they're generally lighter, stronger, water resistant, less prone to rot and better able to withstand difficult and extreme environments.

# LEARNING TO TIE KNOTS

You'll need a couple of lengths of rope of differing colours, about a metre long – this will help you see the knot as it forms – plus a free-standing pole, a 'conventional' wooden chair back or a table leg for tying knots to.

The only way to learn how to tie knots is to practise. Have a go at tying a number of knots. If you're stuck on one, don't worry, move on and try another. Once you've mastered one type you may then find others easier. If you're left-handed try to learn from someone who's also left-handed – it's difficult to follow someone tying a knot when they use the opposite hand. Also, sit alongside the teacher rather than in front of them, otherwise everything will look confusingly upside-down!

## Following instructions

Follow these steps when learning to tie a knot from a drawing:

- Look at the drawing and trace the various twists, crosses and bends with your eye, from the standing part to the working end, to see how the knot is constructed.
- Now lay your rope on a flat surface and take hold of a point 30cm in from the working end.
- Make the first bend, turn or crossover in the knot and then move along to the next.
- Look at the diagrams of knots and compare your work with them.
- Try each knot using these instructions a few times and then try it from memory. Try again a couple of days later. When you can tie the knot correctly three times in a row you'll probably remember it, especially if you continue to practise it occasionally.

Keep the knot flat and your hands open as you tie the knot. If the knot involves two working ends, work them together from the standing parts to the working ends.

Check the shape of the knot at each stage. Make sure you tighten the knot correctly so that it doesn't form the wrong shape at the last minute. With experience you'll find that many knots are actually made up of combinations of other simple knots. Tying more complex ones is just a matter of tying a series of simple ones!

# COMMON KNOTS

Learning knots is like learning a foreign language: it can be baffling at first but, once learned, knots are rarely forgotten. Practise with rope or string that isn't too thick to ensure you have plenty of flexibility.

### Overhand knot

This very basic knot is a simple 'stopper knot' for temporarily securing the end of a piece of rope to prevent it fraying.

Doubling the rope and then tying the knot will make a quick non-slip loop.

### Figure-of-eight

This is a 'stopper knot' that's unlikely to jam or pull loose. It's also used, when doubled, to tie a loop in a rope.

**1** Form a loop in the end of the rope. Take the working end behind the standing part and back over itself into the open loop.

**2** Finish by pulling both sides of the knot tight. If the knot is correct it'll look like a 'figure of eight'.

### Reef knot

This most common knot is used to tie together two working ends of the same material and size.

**1** Take an end of rope in each hand and lay the left-hand end over the right. Then, using your right hand, take the end from the left down behind the other rope and up to the front again.

**2** Point the ends inwards again. This time take the right-hand one over the other, then take it down behind it and up to the front through the loop that has now been formed.

**3** Pull the knot tight. Remember 'left over right and right over left'.

## Caring for rope

Anyone who has spent any time trying to untangle a ball of string will know the importance of caring properly for rope. Coiling your rope takes a little more time than stuffing it into a box, but it will take up less room, ensure it can be used more quickly next time and will also allow you to conduct a visual inspection while you do so. Coil anti-clockwise from the middle of the rope, avoiding contact with the ground as damp and dirt can cause damage.

A number of other dangers can weaken rope – if it is pulled over sharp, rusty or rough edges for example; you should also avoid contact with heat, direct sunlight or chemicals as these will compromise the rope's integrity. Look for signs of wear and tear – frayed strands and yarns. Some damage can be taped or spliced, removing the damaged section. However, if a rope has snapped due to overloading, it should be thrown away.

## Fisherman's knot

Also known as the Improved Clinch knot, it acquired its popular name as it is often used by anglers to tie a hook to a fishing line.

**1** Take two lengths of rope and lay them next to each other.

**2** Tie a thumb knot in the first rope by forming a loop and passing the end through it; pull both ends tight. Tie this around the second rope. Now do the same with the second rope.

**3** Pull both ropes to slide the knots together.

## Sheet bend

A 'sheet' is a sailor's name for a rope. The sheet bend is used to tie together two ropes of different types or unequal thicknesses.

**1** Form a bight in the working end of the thicker rope. Take the working end of the thinner rope and pass it up through the bight.

**2** Take the thinner rope round the back of the bight and trap it under itself. Remember not to take the working end back down the bight in the first rope.

**3** Pull tight by holding the bight in one hand and pulling the standing part of the second rope with the other.

Make sure the two ends are on the same side of the knot. If the ropes are of very different thicknesses, take the working end round the bight and under itself twice to form a double sheet bend.

## Sheepshank

This knot is used to shorten a rope, or to bridge a damaged length, without cutting the rope. It can be tied in the middle of the rope without needing the ends.

**1** Form the rope into an 'S', that is two opposing bights.

**2** In each free end form a half-hitch. Pass the adjacent bight through the half-hitch. Pull the two free ends tight at the same time.

If being used to bridge a damaged portion of rope, make sure the damaged part goes through both half-hitches. That is, the damaged portion should be the centre of the 'S'. The sheepshank should be kept in tension. If loosened it may well come undone.

## Round turn and two half-hitches

This is a long name for a simple hitch used to attach a rope to a post, spar, stake or tree. It's a composite knot formed from two simple knots.

**1** Form a round turn by turning the working end twice around the post.

**2** Then form a half-hitch by taking the working end around the standing part, forming a crossed loop.

**3** Repeat to form a second half-hitch. These should be tied in the same direction and tightened up against the post to ensure that the round turn doesn't slip.

## Clove hitch

The clove hitch is another method of 'hitching' a rope to a post or a rail. Not as secure as the round turn and two half-hitches, it's often used to begin other hitches and lashings.

**1** Pass the working end over and under the post.

**2** Run the working end across the standing part at the front.

**3** Continue round the post again and bring the working end back to trap it under the diagonal.

Thus the two ends of the rope should be laid next to each other under the diagonal but running in opposite directions.

## Highwayman's hitch

This hitch is a 'slip hitch': pulled on the standing end, it holds fast; pulled on the working end, it comes free. Thus it's used to tie a boat to a mooring ring or an animal to a rail or post.

**1** Start by passing a bight behind the post. Take another bight in the standing part and pass it in front of the post and through the first bight.

**2** Then take a third bight in the working end and pass it in front of the post and through the second bight.

**3** Pull tight on the standing part.

### Timber hitch

The timber hitch is a temporary knot used to drag, tow or lift a log or pole. The more strain it is under, the tighter it will grip.

**1** Turn the working end round the standing part and then wrap it around itself at least four or five times.

**2** A half-hitch can be tied in the standing part further up a pole to add some security. The pole is dragged by pulling the standing end.

### Knot safety

Climbing is the most serious application for knots and it is when knots are relied on most – possibly with life-threatening consequences if they aren't properly tied. If you're using a bowline, a stopper knot should also be used to ensure safety. Belayers should also receive exactly the same attention as climbers and the person tying the knot.

### Bowline

The bowline (pronounced 'bo-lin') is used to form a non-slip loop in the end of a rope. It was traditionally the climbers' waist knot before harnesses were used.

**1** Form a loop by passing the working end over the standing part. Pass the working end back up through the loop.

**2** Pass the working end back down the loop and pull tight.

**3** If using synthetic rope, the working end should be locked off against the standing part with a half-hitch.

The bowline is invaluable in rescue situations but might have to be tied blind. So once you're comfortable with tying the knot, practise it with your eyes closed.

### Manharness hitch

Used by hikers and mountaineers to rope themselves together, this knot isn't considered absolutely fail-safe – therefore it shouldn't be used in life-threatening situations.

**1** Loop the rope around itself to create a letter Q with a long tail.

**2** Fold the tail around and fold it around and behind the Q.

**3** Pick up the tail through the centre of the Q and tuck under the bottom of the Q to create a tongue. Pull both ends tight to lengthen the loop.

# LASHINGS

This selection of simple lashings will enable you to construct various items of camp furniture, rafts, bridges and shelters. It is important to keep your lashings as tight as possible so that the resulting structure is safe and secure.

## Square lashing

**1** Begin with a clove hitch underneath the spar to be supported.

**2** Wrap the rope first over one spar, then under the other, pulling tight all the time. On the second time round, go inside the previous turn of rope on top, but outside underneath the spars.

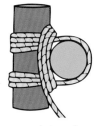

**3** After three turns apply two frapping turns (wrap the rope in the other direction as shown) which pull on the rope turns already made, making them even tighter.

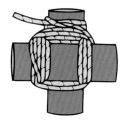

**4** Finish off with a clove hitch.

## Diagonal lashing

**1** Begin with a timber hitch to draw the spars together.

**2** Wrap the rope three times around the spars on the same diagonal as the timber hitch, keeping the rope tight all the time. Wrap three more turns, this time on the other diagonal (at a right angle to the timber hitch).

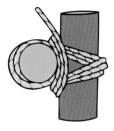

**3** Apply two frapping turns to pull the rope turns tighter.

**4** Finish off with a clove hitch.

# Sheer lashing

**1** It's important to have a good overlap of spars that should be at least a quarter of the length. An overlap of one-third is better still.

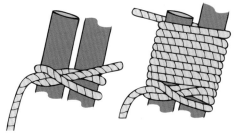

**2** Start with a clove or timber hitch around both spars near the end of the overlap. Continue with eight to ten turns round both spars (or for about 10–15cm).

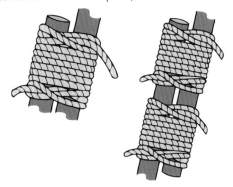

**3** Finish with a clove hitch around the second spar. To tighten, insert small wedges inside the turns. Adding a second lashing will strengthen the overlap, as no movement is then possible in any direction.

# Sheer leg lashing

**1** Line up the two ends or 'butts' of the spars.

**2** Follow step 2 above for the sheer lashing.

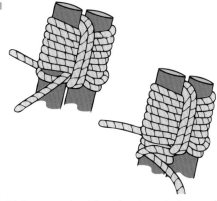

**3** Make a couple of frapping turns between the two spars to tighten the lashings. Finish with a clove hitch.

# Figure-of-eight lashing

This lashing is used to make a tripod. Three spars are laid out with the centre spar lying in the opposite direction to the two outer ones. It's important that the lashing isn't too tight, otherwise the spars cannot move to form the tripod.

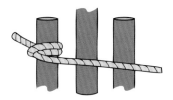

**1** Start with a clove hitch on one of the outside spars.

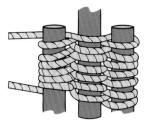

**2** Continue with six or seven turns, which are taken loosely over and under the spars.

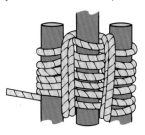

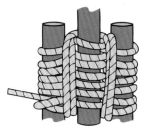

**3** Finish with loose frapping turns and a clove hitch.

**4** Again, wedges can be used to enable even spacing before doing the lashing and frapping turns. The tripod is formed by turning the centre spar through 180° and opening out the two outer spars.

# PROJECT: NETTLE CORDAGE

Nettles are usually remembered as the plant that stung your bare legs as a child. In reality, however, a nettle is an edible plant that has a multitude of uses, of which one of the easiest to make is nettle cordage.

**Difficulty**

**Total time** Allow 1 hour +

**1** Pick the longest nettles you can, taking care to protect your hands. Remove the leaves and stinging hairs (a leather gardening glove and small knife or scissors combine well to achieve this).

**2** Take each stripped stalk and bash its nodes (ie the points where the leaves were) with a stout stick or knife handle – this helps to loosen the inner fibres.

**4** Once the lengthwise slit has been made, take the nettle stem at one end and bend it. This should crack the tough inner core.

**3** Take a knife and slit the nettle from top to bottom, taking care not to cut through to the other side. Once the initial cut is made, a cutlery-type knife or even a thumbnail can often do this job.

**5** It should then be easy to peel the outer part of the nettle away from the inner core. Do this slowly and pay particular attention when pulling over the nodes.

**6** With care you should get some good lengths off. Leave them to dry for a day or, if needed sooner, a couple of hours near a gentle heat source (eg a small campfire).

**8** Take the lower strand of the two and twist it upwards a couple of times, then take it over the top of the upper strand. Repeat this process. You can add in extra nettle, but start twisting in the next lengths well before the end; also, stagger where the joins are, because the cordage will be weaker if they're added at the same spot.

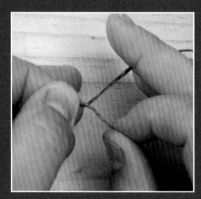

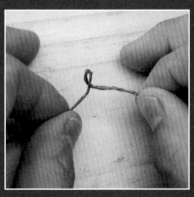

**7** To make cordage, hold a length near the middle and gently twist it in opposite directions until a small loop forms. Pinch the loop between your finger and thumb to hold it.

**9** Got stung? As well as the classic dock leaf, plantain is a very good leaf to use on stings. Check for allergies before using.

# PROJECT:
# PARACORD BRACELET

Paracord is so-called because it's used for parachutes, but it's also a very versatile elasticated cord for craft use, suited to making things as diverse as a wristwatch strap or a woggle. This project shows you how to make a bracelet for less than £1.

To tie all the stages shown in this project for a simple no-frills bracelet, you use a straight-forward knotting method called the cobra weave, which is basically an overhand knot. The cords pictured use hobby shop materials and jute string.

To make the bracelet you'll need some basic tools: sharp scissors to get a clean cut and a lighter to seal the ends; pliers can also be useful to finish off the weave if your ends become short in the final stages. However, to save the fiddle of finishing off with pliers, it's recommended that you start off with a little more paracord than you think you'll need.

First, make a paracord loop to loosely fit your wrist and tie an overhand knot near the end, leaving 3cm or so spare for any adjustment. The knot should fit through the end of the loop when on your wrist. To make things a little clearer in the pictures, a rather smaller knotted loop has been used.

Measure the distance between the end of the loop and the knot – the ratio of paracord to weave length is approximately 30cm to 2.5cm – and then you're ready to start making your bracelet.

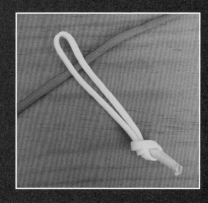

**1** Once you have measured and cut the paracord required for the weave, find the middle and put it behind the loop just down from the top. This small loop is for

the knot to fit snugly through.
**2** Take one length of the paracord (in this case the upper one) and pass it over the front of the loop to the

other side.
**3** Take the other side of the lower paracord length and lay it over the first length.

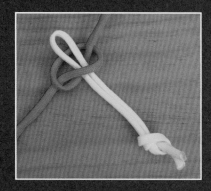

**4** Then take the lower length underneath the back of the loop and through the small gap created by the first length.

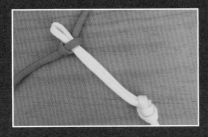

**5** Pull the paracord length tight to complete the first part of the weave.

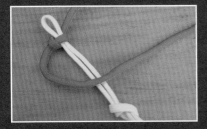

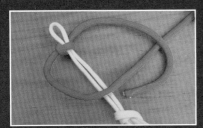

**6** Repeat the weave starting from the other side and alternate thereafter until done. Make sure the weave is neat and compact. You can check that the knot still fits snugly through the loop after a couple of knots because it'll still be possible to adjust it.

**7** Trim off the excess close to the bracelet and melt the end using a lighter. You don't usually need to put the flame actually on the end; very close up will do the job – and excess heat will scorch and blacken the cord. Then make it into a 'paracord rivet' by using the body of the lighter to squash the end. But take care – melted nylon stays hot for some time. This procedure is easier if you use two press-button lighters: the manual type will hurt your thumb after a while, and the metal at the top of a lighter gets hot with extended use. Alternatively the ends can be pulled through the weave on the underside to finish off, but doing this is fiddly.

So, can you think of a specific Scouting use for an elasticated paracord project? Yes, a woggle!

The cobra weave can be used to create a basic framework that's ideal for not only a woggle but also a really appealing, sturdy key ring. Make a loop to the desired length, tie the knot as shown with the red cordage in the photo below, and then weave – a sort of dead-end cobra weave.

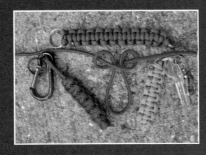

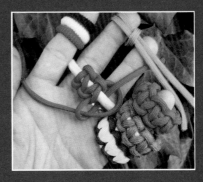

To finish your woggle, simply fold the loop around a suitably sized broom handle or similar, tie the end into the knot and weave. It's a bit tight to start off, but once secured slip it off the broom handle and finish it. This technique can also be used to make two-colour woggles.

Using a couple of smaller elasticated hairbands works a treat when making a woggle.

Paracord is thick enough to hold watches and also compasses (there are special compasses for such use). You can also add split rings or karabiners as you see fit.

And why stop at paracord? You can use anything from natural grasses to guy lines. You can also make things out of 'gutted' paracord, but bear in mind that the useful inner strands will then be missing and that you'll need a greater length to weave with, as it's thinner.

As mentioned, always allow a little more paracord when making things; but what to do with the offcuts? Soak them in PVA and snip them into beads!

# PIONEERING
# AND GADGETS

Pioneering is the process of designing and constructing equipment for practical uses. This can range from a simple washstand for your bowl to a rope bridge across a river.

## The essentials of pioneering

The history of pioneering goes right back to the time when people first started to build structures. The construction of Stonehenge doubtless employed pioneering techniques to manoeuvre its massive stones into place, and you'll still see 'scaffolding' made in the pioneering style when you travel around various parts of the world today.

Pioneering requires a familiarity with knots and lashings and their appropriate use. As a minimum an ability to tie square, diagonal and sheer lashing will be needed as these are the mainstay of all rope work in pioneering projects. With more ambitious projects, teamwork and forward planning are also necessary.

A range of equipment will be needed including rope, spars and often pulleys. Spars can be bought from garden centres, timber merchants or the Forestry Commission, and ropes and pulleys from ships' chandlers.

Rope comes in many sizes and is typically measured by its circumference, but as a simple guide 75mm or larger (about the diameter of a broom handle) should be used to hold weight on projects like monkey bridges and aerial runways and for foot and hand rails; 50mm rope (about the thickness of a thumb) should be used for pulleys, making rope ladders and when anchoring structures;

and 25mm rope (about the thickness of an index finger) can be used for guy lines on smaller projects and non-weight-bearing lashings.

The poles or spars need to be sturdy and must be checked before use. Poles that have lain on the ground could have become damp, which may have caused them to rot. A simple test is to let one end of the pole drop on to a hard surface. It should have a solid 'ring' to it when it hits the floor and will bounce a little. If the sound is a dull thud and there's no bounce it means the spar is probably unsafe for use.

Of course, you can start with much smaller projects which can be put together at home using bamboo canes and elastic bands – this is often a good way of 'rehearsing' a bigger project to get an idea of how much equipment is needed and the amount of work that would be involved.

# TRIPOD STAND

Tripod stands can perform various useful camping functions, the most common being to suspend a cooking pot over a fire or to provide a washstand.

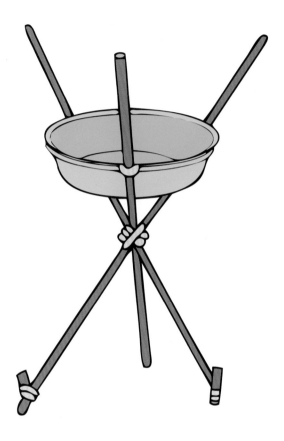

**1** To make a tripod cooking pot stand, tie the upper ends of three poles together using a figure-of-eight or tripod lashing (see page 123).

**2** To create a variable pot hook for the stand you'll need a strong piece of wood with several upward-angled branches. Strip off the bark to ensure there's no rot to weaken the wood, then cut the branches to about 10cm stumps. Lash the hook to hang from the top of the tripod stand. Test the hook for strength before you light the fire and suspend a pot full of food from it!

**3** Alternatively, to make a tripod washstand lash the three poles together lower down, roughly in the middle, at a convenient height to hold a bowl. Tie a rope around the rim of the bowl to secure it to the tripod.

**4** To provide any tripod stand with additional stability, lash its feet to wooden pegs pushed into the ground.

# WALLS AND SCREENS

Fences and walls aren't only a way of providing your camp with windbreaks, shelters and privacy (in toilet or washing areas), they're also useful to reflect the heat of a campfire back towards you.

**1** Push two pairs of sticks into the ground a stick's width apart. Fill the vertical gap between them with more sticks laid horizontally, and lash the upright poles together at the top to hold things in place.

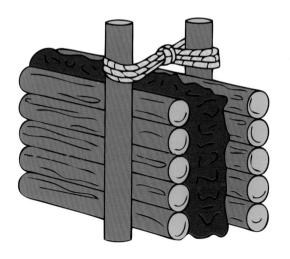

**2** Alternatively, to create a stronger fence leave more space between each pair of uprights, line the gap with two rows of horizontal poles and pile earth between them.

# CHAIR

This simple camp chair is a great way to take the weight off your feet. Depending on the strength of your lashings, you may find it a little wobbly; if so, add bracing at the back as described in step 6.

## Materials

- 11 x stout staves 0.9m (3ft)
- 10 x stout staves 1.2m (4ft)
- 30 light lashings

## Method

**1** The two side frames are built first using four 1.2m staves for each. The seat support bars need to be 0.45m (18in) up from the bottom of the uprights.

**2** Next, join the side frames using four 0.9m staves.

**3** Another 0.9m stave is lashed to the seat support 0.2m in front of the back tie.

**4** Lash two 1.2m staves in place to support the back of the seat.

**5** Use the remaining 0.9m staves to form the seat and back rest.

**6** If necessary, stabilise by lashing some diagonal bracing between the back legs.

# TABLE

Your table can be any height you like – big enough to prepare food on or just a small coffee table. You'll need nine staves all the same length plus two short ones for bracing.

## Materials

- 9 x medium staves
- 2 x short staves
- 3 x long staves

## Method

**1** Prepare two identical side frames.

**2** Join them with a further three longitudinal staves.

**3** Brace using diagonal ties from each end of the lower longitudinal stave to the centre of the top of the frame opposite.

**4** The table top can be made of staves, wood or whatever is available.

# TABLE AND BENCHES

An ideal project for a small team or Patrol, the team can then celebrate their success by enjoying a lunch together. For evening dining, a light could be hung from the central apex.

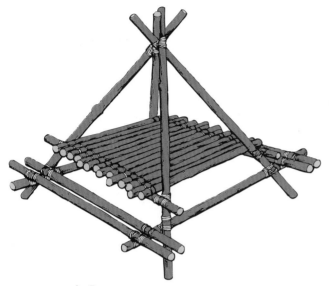

## Materials
- 4 x spars 3.6m (12ft)
- 6 x spars 3m (10ft)
- 2 x spars 2m (6ft)
- Approximately 20 light spars
- Sisal or light rope

## Method

**1** Construct two A-frames.

**2** Lean the two A-frames together and join them with two 3m spars, which need to rest on the cross members of the A-frames.

**3** Two 2m spars are lashed between the A-frames to act as supports for the tabletop.

**4** The last two 3m spars are lashed alongside the spars joining the A frames, to form the bench seats.

**5** Light spars are used for the tabletop and tied in place with sisal or light rope.

# CAMP DRESSER

Keep your camp kitchen in order! This impressive dresser should be large enough to accommodate a washing-up bowl with enough space left over to allow your entire dinner service to drip dry.

## Materials
- 6 x staves 1.8m (6ft)
- 2 x staves 0.5m (1.6ft)
- Sisal
- 2 x pegs
- Roll-top table or more short staves

## Method

**1** Select the two straightest staves for the worktop. Using the remaining staves, make two identical A-frames, ensuring the horizontal bars are at waist height. Use a sheer lashing at the top and square lashings on the horizontal staves.

**2** Lash the other long staves on top of the short horizontal staves using square lashings. If you're using a roll-top table, make sure that it'll sit on these staves without falling through. If you have a square or rectangular washing-up bowl it can be supported in the dresser by two additional short staves.

**3** The rest of the dresser should be covered with either the tabletop or more short staves.

**4** To ensure that the dresser is quite stable, drive a peg into the ground at each end and run a guy line from one peg, across the A-frames to the other peg. Secure the guy line to the pegs with the mooring hitch or round turn and two half hitches, and to the A-frames with clove hitches.

# FIRES, FOOD AND COOKING

Heat, light and warmth are basic human needs. It's therefore vital that everyone who ventures into the Great Outdoors knows how to build a good fire. You don't have to be a master of the art of firelighting – waterproof matches or a simple flint will suffice – but being able to light a fire in a variety of conditions remains essential. The size and type of fire you build depends on what you want to use it for: warmth, cooking, or providing the focal point of an entertainment. Whatever you build, you must do it safely and with due consideration to the impact you have on the land. Don't dig a hole in the ground unless you have permission from the landowner.

# FIRES AND FIRELIGHTING

Firelighting is an art, but like any artist you need good-quality equipment and materials to get the best results. Preparation is all and will pay dividends on a cold, wet night when you need your fire the most.

## Tinder, kindling and fuel

There are three essential ingredients for firelighting – tinder, kindling and fuel wood – and it's a good idea to collect a worthwhile supply of all three before lighting your fire. Grade the materials in order of thickness. You can then feed the fire slowly and gradually, which should give the best results.

## Tinder

This is the small, dry, highly combustible material used to start a fire. Examples include wood shavings, crumbled rotten wood (also called punk), dried grass, birch bark, leaves, string and even fungus such as crampballs (also called King Alfred's cakes as they resemble burnt buns). Tinder is used primarily to catch a flame, but your choice of tinder will relate to how you light the fire. For example, if you have a lighter then birch bark is a good choice. If using a bow drill, bracken and grass are better.

*Dried grass is an excellent tinder; a flame can be coaxed with small pieces of fungus.*

## Kindling

Once you have a spark and flame you need material to keep the fire going. Kindling normally consists of small sticks and splinters (think of the thickness ranging from a match up to a pencil), larger than tinder but not yet logs or large pieces of wood. Of course, your kindling needs to be bone dry too. Be careful not to smother your fire with too much, or too large, too soon.

## Fuel

For most campfires, medium-sized sticks and logs (up to the maximum thickness of your arm) are fine for fuel. These should be laid on carefully, or built as part of the construction of your fire, ensuring you don't put the fire out at the same time. Although ideally your fuel wood should be dry, it can be a little damp, as the fire will dry it out before it catches. Never use live or green wood.

## Ferro rod

Much more reliable than matches, a flint and steel set will stand you in good stead for many camping trips. It's the best way to guarantee a spark in the very wettest of conditions. However, a spark isn't much good if you've nothing to catch – see the section on kindling materials.

## Lighters

There are many different kinds of lighter available, from the cheap disposable types used by smokers to storm-proof varieties. A cheap lighter will be fine in fair conditions, but will prove less reliable in strong wind and rain. For more effective results a so-called storm-proof lighter is recommended. These use butane and have a more sophisticated delivery mechanism.

## Waterproof matches

Rather like something from a James Bond novel, the waterproof match was originally developed for the Ministry of Defence; the flame cannot be blown out and the matches will still light even when wet. They're available from good outdoor equipment retailers.

## Using the sun

Begin by preparing your tinder. Pile up some crumbled leaves in a dry place away from other sources of ignition. Now, using a magnifying glass, focus the sun's rays into a circle on a spot in the centre, making the circle as small and round as possible. Smoke and flame should follow.

# CAMPFIRE FOUNDATIONS

The campfire is the focal point of a camp and many memorable times will be spent around it – cooking, singing or talking. But ensure you prepare carefully.

**1** Using a spade, cut through the turf to mark the outline of your fireplace. Then divide the area into smaller squares.

**2** Slide the spade or knife under each small square and lift it away. Store the squares away from the fire, grassy side down, and water them regularly to prevent them from drying out.

**3** Establish the perimeter of the fireplace by edging or 'banking' the cleared area with large stones, logs, bricks or mounds of soil. This banking will contain the fire and its ashes, to keep it from spreading and protect it from the wind. Space the stones out a little so that air can be drawn into the base of the fire.

# TYPES OF FIRE

The type and size of fire you build should depend on the materials you have available, the purpose of the fire (will you be cooking a three-course dinner or just boiling water?) and also personal preference. Here are some of the most common fire types, all of which are reasonably easy to build, to light and to maintain.

### Ground fire with tower

This is an excellent fire to use when the ground mustn't be scorched, dug or otherwise disturbed. There are many variations on the theme, but one of the simplest is to make a single- or double-layered platform using similar-sized logs. Then create a top level made of smaller sticks also lashed together. Ensuring the whole contraption is sturdy, cover it with soil to prevent the altar itself catching alight. Then make your fire on top.

### Star fire

This is a way of making a fire using kindling and small sticks. Make a conical shape from this material, then push in the ends of six slender logs around the fire to create a star shape. These logs will act as fuel, so the fire will burn for a long time. As the fire burns down, push these logs in towards the centre.

### Trench fire

Dig a rectangular hole in the ground measuring approximately a metre long by 30cm wide and 30cm deep. The base of the hole should be at a gentle slope ending at ground level on an angle of approximately 20°. Keep the back wall of the fire facing into the wind to supply it with air. You can lay a grate across the top for cooking. This type of fire is particularly effective in windy conditions.

### Crane fire

Find two stout sticks of different lengths, each with a fork, and push them into the ground as shown. Then find a longer stick to rest on these forks. Using a steel hook you can now suspend a billycan to hang above your fire.

## Wigwam fire

As its name suggests, this takes the form of a wigwam or tepee shape and is the classic campfire. To make it, find a large stick and embed it in the ground. Surround it with a couple of handfuls of small kindling. Now lean a series of smaller sticks against the central stick all the way around. Repeat with larger sticks to create another layer, ensuring you leave enough space for air to circulate. Light the fire in the centre then blow as necessary until it catches.

## Reflector fire

This works on the principle of directing heat back towards the fire. In order for this to happen you need to make a screen of wood or stone to act as a reflector. One of the easiest methods is to build the screen behind the fire from logs laid on top of each other.

# FINDING A FIREPLACE

Fires can cause damage! Think carefully about the location of your fire and – importantly – the effect it will have on the ground.

### At a campsite

If you're staying at a commercial campsite it's unlikely that you'll be allowed to light an open fire. However, if an open fire is permitted, there's likely to be a designated area. This should be a level area with plenty of space, reasonably close (but not too close) to a good source of fuel. If you're in any doubt about whether you can light a fire, speak to the landowner. Don't light a fire on grass.

### In the countryside

The impact of a poor location for your fire can be disastrous, particularly in very dry conditions. Light your fire well away from trees and hedgerows and look for a spot where a fire has been started before. Always get permission for your fire from the landowner.

# PROJECT: GROUND FIRE WITH TOWER

This is a very practical way to prepare a fire for cooking in foil at backwoods type camps – baked potatoes, egg in a potato and chocolate bananas can all be cooked in its embers.

**Difficulty**     **Total time** Allow 20 minutes

First find a suitable spot away from combustible materials and preferably rock free. An existing fire scar could be used, but if not then prepare an area by removing turfs and set aside for reuse (always get the campsite's permission before doing this).

## The 'FLAMES' method

This won't fail so long as the directions are followed. Just remember the acronym FLAMES:

**F** — Find a suitable place to build your fire.

**L** — Look for and prepare your hearth.

**A** — Assemble your Baskerville burner.

**M** — Make your fire.

**E** — Engage your spark and light your fire.

**S** — Sustain your fire.

**1** Lay a hearth of timber roughly 50cm in diameter preferably seasoned/dry. This can be determined by weight and colour, and also by a simple scrape test of the bark.

**2** Now start to build a tower with dry sticks roughly the diameter of a thumb (2cm) and 40cm square. Build this up to a height of about 10cm.

**3** Now fill this with your tinder/kindling fuzz sticks, birch twigs no bigger than a pencil lead, cotton wool, paper etc.

**4** Continue to build the tower up with dry sticks of reducing size to a height of approx 40cm.

**5** Now light your fire and leave to burn down. By the time it has burnt down the hearth should be glowing nicely ready for your baked potatoes.

**6** The size of this fire depends on how many going to cook on it. Remember cook on embers not flames.

# PROJECT: STAR FIRE

This fire lay is an easy and practical way to build a fire for cooking with a pot or pan. The logs placed in the star configuration give a stable base on which to rest the pan once the fire has burnt down to embers.

**Difficulty**

**Total time** Allow 20 minutes

Choose an area well away from overhanging trees or other material which may catch fire and clear of rocks. If you can't find an existing fire scar, prepare the fire base by removing turfs and set these aside for reuse (don't forget to seek the landowner's permission before you start).

## Time for a brew?

You can use the arrangement below to create a secure crane above your fire from which to hang a camp kettle. Simply create two vertical props, forked at the end and lay a crossbar over the top. The kettle is then suspended on a stick of the right length with notches cut into either end. Remember to let the fire burn down first, so you do not scorch the bottom of your kettle.

**1** Before you start to build your fire, it is a good idea to collect sticks and logs and sort them roughly by size. You will then have everything you need to hand rather than having to hunt for more sticks as you go.

**2** Take six timbers roughly 7cm thick and lay them in a star shape. Use preferably seasoned/dry wood; this can be determined by weight and colour and also a simple scrape test of the bark.

**3** Build a tripod over the centre of the star. Proceed to build a tipi shape with dry twigs about finger thick (don't forget to give them a snap test to prove they are dry – they should break easily with a dry 'snap').

**6** The fire steel (ferrocerium rod) is a great way to light a fire with just a spark. The larger 10mm-size rods tend to be easier to handle, creating bigger sparks and giving more success.

**4** Leave one side open and fill this with your tinder/kindling fuzz sticks, peelings of silver birch bark, cotton wool, paper and so on.

**7** Now light your fire and leave to burn down. By the time it has burnt down, the centre of the star should be glowing nicely ready for your pot or pan. Remember to cook on embers not flames.

**5** Now add additional twigs and sticks from the size of a pencil lead up to little finger size and contine to build the tipi, ensuring that you leave a gap so that you can light the tinder in the centre.

**8** Check the logs as they burn, feed the timber forming the star towards the fire therefore refuelling it as it burns. You should also have extra logs ready in case they are needed.

# FIRELIGHTING
# TIPS AND TRICKS

Picking up firelighting skills is much like learning magic – what initially seems quite mysterious is revealed to be quite straightforward. Learn some of these tricks and you will always stay warm in the Great Outdoors.

## How to make fire out of water

If you really want to impress, how about making fire from water? This takes a lot of practice and patience but it does work.

Put a sheet of cling film in a mug. Half fill the mug and gently lift the cling film, wrapped around the water, to form a water crystal ball. Under bright sunlight hold this crystal ball over your dark-coloured tinder, moving it up and down like a lens until you beam a bright dot of light on to the tinder. Wear sunglasses to protect your eyes.

## How to make fire from ice

Break a reasonably thick piece of ice from a river or stream (up to 6cm depth is ideal). Carefully, using a knife or saw, scrape away any dirt or imperfections and begin to form it into a circle. Use the heat from your bare hands to help melt the ice into a disc, turning it to prevent your hands from becoming too cold. Once your ice is ready, wedge it securely on its side in an elevated position between the sun and your tinder (crumbled, dried leaves for example). Angle the ice so that the sun forms a small circle on the tinder. The tinder should light in dramatic fashion – so stand well back!

### Fuzz stick

Choose a dry stick around 2–3cm in diameter. Now, using your knife, slice down the stick's sides making sure that they remain attached. The idea is that the these thin shavings are easier to light than the main stick. If you create a number of fuzz sticks and place them in amongst your larger fuel, this will be an effective way of starting your fire.

## How to make fire from a drinks can

After you've drained the last dregs of your fizzy pop, don't throw away the can (you should recycle it anyway) – the base can be used as a parabolic mirror to train sunlight on your fuel source.

The first thing you need to do is increase the reflective surface by rubbing the base of the can for a few minutes with steel wool (toothpaste works too). Keep polishing until you can see your face in the base.

Now hold up the bottom of the can towards the sun. On the end of a small piece of wood, place a tiny bit of bone dry dark-coloured tinder. Given enough sunlight, the tinder will begin to smoke. You'll need to experiment moving the end of the stick closer to and further from the can to get the optimum heat from the sun, but about 5cm distance is considered best.

Alternatively, take your torch apart and use the reflector. Remove the bulb and poke the tinder through the hole where the bulb was.

## Dry kindling

If you have no dry kindling in wet weather, go to the nearest hedge. You can always find dry, dead wood for starting a fire in the thickest part of the hedge; but take care not to damage the hedge itself as you retrieve your dry kindling from the middle of it.

## Make an outdoor candle holder

Find a strip of bark about 10–12cm long and 3–4cm wide (silver birch is good). Alternatively use thin card.

Find a stick about 3cm diameter and split the end in the middle, down about 6cm.

Wrap the bark or card around the candle and slot into the slit. If the slit is too wide, tie a couple or turns of cord around the top of the stick.

## Make your own firelighting kit

A pencil sharpener comes into its own out in the wild – simply find a stick around the same thickness as a pencil and sharpen it in the normal way. The shavings produced are ideal tinder. Also make sure you pack a thin metal tube to act as a blowpipe to get oxygen to your fire. Remember that this could get hot – so be warned. Finally, why not carry some pine cones fitted with a string wick and dipped in candle wax. These are fine standby firelighters.

## King Alfred's Cake

One of the strangest natural firelighters is a fungas called *Daldinia concentrica* and also known as crampballs. It is found on dead wood (especially ash). At first glance, it looks like a lump of coal but has been most associated with the cakes King Alfred (849–899) was said to have burnt when hiding out in the country. The black variety are best for firelighting (and it must be perfectly dry). A spark is enough to ignite it and it will burn for a considerable time.

# BASKERVILLE BURNER

The Baskerville burner is a fire that resembles a rocket. It was 'invented' in 1989 when instructors at Tolmers Scout Camp kept burning their fingers whilst trying to light pine cones. One of them had the bright idea of standing the cone on three twigs. Then he stuffed birch bark into the pine cone and found he had a brilliant firelighter that can be used anywhere.

You'll need to collect the natural materials, build the fire around the burner, dig and form the hearth, then light and sustain the fire.

Most campsites have plenty of silver birch available, but you can also collect it from the ground in most woodland. Dry pine cones can be found beneath most fir trees. Firewood can be collected from the floor of most wooded areas, but ensure that it's dry.

**1** Tear the bark into strips about as wide as a fingernail and fold the strips over.

**2** Stuff the strips into the bottom of the pine cone and continue until all the leaves of the pine cone are stuffed with birch bark.

**3** Break the twig into three and stand the burner up.

**4** Surround the burner with small twigs and other kindling.

**5** Light the bottom of the burner.

# PROJECT:
# BOW DRILL

The bow drill is a method of making fire using the friction between two pieces of wood. Common woods considered ideal for making fire this way include willow, hazel, alder and lime. The bow drill kit itself comprises five components plus a tinder bundle.

**Difficulty**           **Total time** 5–10 minutes

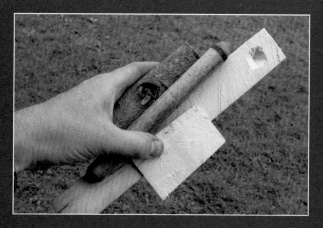

**1** The drill used here is hazel, about the thickness of an adult's thumb. It should be straight and round, with both ends pointed, one end being stubby and the other tapered. The baseboard is made of lime about 2cm thick and the drill rotates in a round depression carved with a knife. A good test for any drill and baseboard wood is that you can push your thumbnail into it and leave a shallow impression.

The top of the drill sits inside another depression in a green-wood bearing block, which is filled with leaves to reduce friction. The bearing block is used to hold the drill in place and apply pressure when necessary.

In the final stages an ember pan is used to collect hot wood dust; this is typically a sliver of wood or bark (not silver birch, as it can curl).

The drill is turned by a wooden bow about chest to fingertip in length, slightly curved, with little flex and a V-shaped notch in both ends to hold the cordage (paracord in this instance). If you hear a squeaking sound at any stage, it could be that the surfaces are getting polished (it's also a possible sign of moisture). To correct this, simply cut across the end of the drill to roughen it up a little – don't re-cut it, as this removes the carbonised material.

**2** Attach the bow to the drill as shown. Put your foot on the base board at the opposite end to the depression and locate the drill's stubby point in it. Place the bearing block on the tapered end. Start drilling slowly and steadily, as the aim at the moment is to bed in the drill and char the depression.

**3** Once in your stride you should see thin wisps of smoke emanating and some cool charred dust should form. At this stage the depression should be charred too.

**4** Once the baseboard charring is achieved, cut a 1/8th segment out of the depression using a knife (and a folding saw if necessary), making sure the segment walls are smooth and straight in order to maximise the amount of hot dust falling through.

**5** Making sure the ember pan is directly under the notch to collect the dust, mount the drill as before and slowly start to turn it. After a while smoke should noticeably issue and twirl up the drill, along with more powder pushing out of the notch. At this point, start to smoothly increase your bow rate whilst applying a little more bearing block pressure. After 10–20 or so good strokes lift the still-mounted drill to check the powder. If it's ready to form an ember it'll sustain its own smoke. If not, bow some more until it is. Gently ease it out of the baseboard notch with a blade or thin stick, and let it develop. If the ground is damp, cup it in your hands, and at this stage you mustn't blow on it or leave it where the wind can blow it – gentle wafts of the hand will suffice if needed. When it can be seen glowing strongly you've got a usable ember.

**6** Your prepared tinder bundle will typically be a mix of things like dried bracken, grass and buffed clematis bark, and remember it's worth gathering more than you think you'll need.

**7** To help it along, things like downy seeds, birch bark or a piece of dried cramp ball fungus (Daldinia Concentrica) can be placed in the middle to receive the ember. Hold the tinder bundle in one hand at a slight angle, place the ember pan near the middle and gently tip the ember into the centre whilst tipping the tinder bundle level, as this will help to protect the ember. Make sure that the ember is secure to a maximum of a third of the way in and in good contact with the tinder, but not so tight as to starve it of oxygen.

**8** If there's any breeze, turn so that it's behind you and blow into the bundle from about 15cm away (any closer and the moisture in your breath will come into play). You need sustained firm breaths, as you're trying to get oxygen in, not blow a fly off your arm. When you need to draw breath avoid inhaling smoke.

**9** As you progress you should hear crackle sounds, see smoke issue and then flames, and often if the smoke is thick it changes to a slightly creamy/green colour just before igniting.

With thanks to **Dale Collett**
www.learnbushcraft.co.uk

# PROJECT: PENNY STOVE

How do you make a cup of tea from a can of cola? With just two tin cans and a supply of methylated spirit you can produce a functioning miniature stove. Not only does it save money on buying a new one, it's fun to do – and a way to recycle.

**Difficulty**

**Total time** Allow 20 minutes

These instructions will enable you to create a basic penny stove from two 330ml drinks cans. If you're feeling adventurous then a more advanced version can be made which incorporates a trimmed-down section placed snugly inside from a smaller can (eg a small tonic/mixer can inside the two 330ml can parts). Slots need to be cut into the small-can insert at the bottom and this forms a wall that allows the methylated spirit to flow between it and the can walls to the burner holes, which increases the pressure.

## Tool list

- Cork board pin
- Thin pliers
- Small hammer
- Scissors or craft knife
- Sandpaper
- Medium-sized nail
- 1p coin (penny)
- Chopping board or old piece of wood

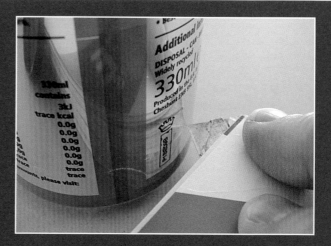

**1** Use scissors or a craft blade secured in a book to cut down two drinks can bottoms to about 2.5cm in height (but make one a couple of millimetres or so smaller than the other). Sand the resulting sharp edges, as this will make slotting them together a bit easier. The cans are fairly safe to handle when cut and sanded, but do still take care. If using scissors then the cut can become a bit tight, so make angled cuts once or twice to ease the tension.

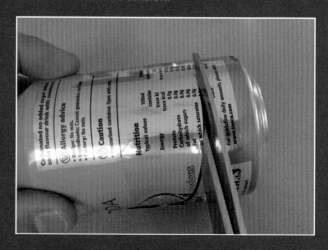

**2** These are the two halves. The burners look great sanded down. Pack out with newspaper or similar if you sand the cut sections before you start, as they're very thin. Sanding is best done whilst they're still unopened.

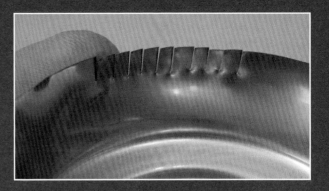

**5** Or make a series of small cuts around the rim and crimp all the way round. Gently slide together, with the smaller one sliding over the larger. The reason the smaller one goes on top is that it will not reach the full height of the one at the bottom (ie the inner one) when pushed together and therefore the edge can't sit proud.

**3** Take the slightly smaller section and, using a cork board pin and small hammer, knock six to eight holes equally into the rim and use a small nail to make one hole in the centre of the concave base.

**6** The meths will need priming, which means it needs warming to get the penny stove to work properly. Make a priming reservoir out of a large metal lid or wrap some gauze around the middle and soak it.

**4** Gently push a spare full tin into the slightly smaller can bottom, as this eases the rim open slightly. Push too hard and the side will split, which will render it useless. Put a small crimp in the other (slightly larger) can bottom's rim.

**7** Fill the cooker with meths through the central hole and then cover it with a penny – this helps to build the internal pressure and prevents the very small chance of the flame getting sucked into the cooker.

# BURNING PROPERTIES OF WOOD

The burning properties described here assume that you're using dry, seasoned wood.
All woods burn better when seasoned and some burn better when split rather than as whole logs.

**Alder**
Poor in heat and doesn't last.

**Apple**
Splendid. It burns slowly and steadily with little flame but good heat. The scent is also pleasing.

**Ash**
The best burning wood, providing both flame and heat, and if necessary will burn when green.

**Beech**
A rival to ash, though not as good and only fair when green.

**Birch**
The heat is good but it burns quickly. The smell is pleasant.

**Blackthorn**
Quite one of the best woods. Burns slowly, with good heat and little smoke.

**Cedar**
Needs to be fully dried. Full of snap and crackle. It gives little flame but much heat and the scent is beautiful.

**Cherry**
Burns slowly with good heat. Another wood with the advantage of a pleasant scent.

**Douglas fir**
Little flame or heat.

**Elder**
Mediocre. A very smoky quick burner with not much heat.

**Elm**
Unpredictable since Dutch elm disease. Can, but doesn't always, smoke violently. One large log put on before bed will keep the fire burning until morning.

**Hawthorn**
Similar to blackthorn.

**Hazel**
Good.

**Holly**
Good only when seasoned.

**Hornbeam**
Almost as good as beech.

**Horse chestnut**
Good flame and heating power but spits a lot.

**Larch**
Crackly, scented and fairly good for heat.

**Laurel**
Has a brilliant flame.

**Lime**
Poor. Burns with a dull flame.

**Maple**
Good.

**Oak**
Sparse flame and the smoke is acrid. Very old dry seasoned oak is excellent for heat, burning slowly and steadily and producing little ash.

**Pear**
A good heat and a good scent.

**Pine**
Burns with a splendid flame, but is apt to spit. The resinous Weymouth pine has a lovely scent and a cheerful blue flame.

**Plane**
Burns pleasantly but can throw sparks if very dry.

**Plum**
Good heat and scent.

**Poplar**
Poor to fair.

**Rhododendron**
The thick old stems, being very tough, burn well.

**Robinia (acacia)**
Burns slowly with good heat but with acrid smoke.

**Spruce**
Burns too quickly and with too many sparks.

**Sycamore**
Burns with a good flame and moderate heat.

**Walnut**
Good with a pleasant scent.

**Willow**
Poor. Burns slowly with little flame even when seasoned, and is apt to spark.

**Yew**
Last but one of the best. Burns slowly with a fierce heat and the scent is pleasant.

# CAMPFIRE SAFETY

If not properly controlled your campfire is potentially dangerous both to people and the natural habitat. Fire spreads quickly and a stray ember can sometimes be enough to start a forest fire. Familiarise yourself with these simple safety measures to ensure your campfire is a safe and happy one.

## Extinguishing a campfire

Ideally the fire should be allowed to burn down – simply stop adding fuel and wait for it to turn to ash. Break up any large logs with a stick so that they burn more quickly. Once reduced to ash, pour water on all parts of the fire, stirring with a stick to ensure that the water reaches all of it. Check no stray embers have escaped. Add more water, and finally, before leaving the site, carefully check that the ashes are cold to the touch.

## Clearing away a fireplace

If you're leaving the campsite altogether you must clear away the fireplace too. In a wilderness area, leave as little trace of it as possible. Dig over the fireplace to make sure there are no ashes left on the surface. Scatter fresh soil over it, then smooth it down and water it well. Replace any cut turf and fill in gappy edges with soil, grass and leaves to look as natural as possible.

## Wildfires

Accidental and uncontrolled fires can cause as much damage to wildlife and habitats as to people and property. Take particular care with matches at all times of year, not only during dry summers. Sometimes vegetation is deliberately fired in some fields, heaths and moors between October and early April, so always check that a fire isn't supervised before calling 999.

## Safety checklist

☑ Never leave a fire unattended.

☑ Be aware of the time of year and any regulations for the area in which you're camping. Is the area prone to bush fires in dry summers, for example? Or are there protected species of trees or plants nearby?

☑ Never use methylated spirits, paraffin, petrol or other chemicals to start or rekindle a fire. These liquids are very volatile, and if the vapour from them catches alight you could be caught in the flames.

☑ Don't build a fire bigger than you need, and be aware of the direction and strength of the wind. Wind can make a fire flare up and blow sparks that could set light to other areas.

☑ Don't use riverbed rocks or flint to line or edge your fireplace, as they've been known to explode when they get hot.

☑ Take care when using a fire within or near a shelter. Sparks or exploding embers could burn you or your clothing.

☑ Do not bury hot ashes or coals; although this may seem a neat solution, you may set light to roots causing fires to spread both under and over ground.

# WAYS OF COOKING

There are lots of ways to cook food, even when you're camping. Decide beforehand which method you're going to use for each food and in what order you will cook. Some foods and methods need more time than others.

## Getting started

Work out what pans you'll need. The fewer pans you have the more inventive you can be (and will need to be) in using them – there's a lot you can do with one-pot cooking. Make sure you have everything to hand before you start, including plenty of fresh water and fuel.

Begin by cleaning and chopping any fresh vegetables or meat and measuring out any dry ingredients so that they're ready to use when you need them.

## Frying

Most people think of frying when they think about camp cooking. Simply put, frying is cooking food in a small amount of hot oil at the bottom of the pan, but it's surprisingly hard to get it right. The difficulty is maintaining an even temperature when there's a lot of food to be cooked and a limited amount of space – there's only so much food that can be cooked in a pan at the same time. What do you do if other food is ready but you can only fry in small batches? Fried food is also rather bad for your health, due to its high fat content.

Stir-frying is more fun, convenient and healthier. Its main cooking advantages are that a wok or similar pan has more space in which to cook and that all your food can be cooked in the same pot. However, think carefully about the order in which you cook your ingredients – meat will take longer than vegetables, for example.

Deep-frying is best avoided on camp. It involves completely covering your food in hot oil, which means you require a considerable quantity of it. Nevertheless, this is one of the tastiest ways of cooking fish and vegetables, and even chocolate bars (which comes with the usual health warning!).

## Baking

Baking is a healthy option and reasonably straightforward in that food can be placed directly into a camp oven. However, bear in mind that if your oven is made from a biscuit tin, it's unlikely to have dials, gauges and timers. This means you'll need to rely on your own judgement and experience when it comes to cooking times. Potatoes can also be wrapped in foil and baked directly on hot embers.

## Grilling

In this form of cooking intense heat is applied either above or below the food. It works well for everything, from bread to fish and thinly sliced meat. However, food cannot be left to grill – you must attend to it at every stage, checking and turning so that it doesn't get overcooked on one side. You'll also need to ensure that food doesn't just look cooked – we should all be familiar by now with 'burnt sausage syndrome', when they're black on the outside but pink (and therefore unsafe) on the inside.

## Campfire cooking

If you don't have the equipment to hold a frying pan over the fire to cook your breakfast, try using three long, green sticks.

Sharpen the ends of the sticks, which should be about 3cm or more in diameter, and flatten the other end. Knock the sticks into the ground over the embers to make a tripod and balance the frying pan on that. (Note: make sure you use green sticks – if you use dry sticks your breakfast will end up on the fire!)

# STOVE OR CAMPFIRE?

Your wood fire or portable stove is at the heart of your outdoor kitchen. While cooking over a wood fire can be great fun and give your food a deliciously smoky flavour, it can also be hard to control temperature and cooking speed. A camp stove, on the other hand, might be a bit less fun but will deliver better results, especially if you're a novice cook.

## Choose a wood fire:

- If there are plenty of you.
- For longer camps in the same location.
- For food that requires a long cooking time.
- When you want to teach or learn backwoods cooking skills.

## Choose a stove:

- If there are only a few of you.
- If you're on the move, for example on a lightweight expedition.
- If there's insufficient wood for a fire.
- If you're in a hurry or there's very little cooking to be done.
- In wet or windy weather.

## Poaching

Fill your pan with water, boil and then simmer just below 100°. Food – particularly fish and eggs – can then be carefully placed in the water (without splashing). If cooking fish, submerge it in lightly salted water and simmer for ten minutes or until it flakes. While cooking eggs, cover the yolks with egg white using a pair of spoons; then cover and cook for ten minutes.

## Stewing

A popular and easy way of preparing a hot meal, usually involving cooking minced or chopped meat plus potatoes and other vegetables. Once the water has come to the boil lower it to a simmer so that the ingredients cook gently, while still ensuring that the liquid continues to bubble. If you have to add cold water or cold ingredients during cooking, take the pan off the heat and let it cool slightly first, otherwise the water will spit and steam.

## Boiling

This simply involves bringing a pan of water to the boil, adding vegetables, rice, pasta or other grains and keeping the water at or just below boiling until the food is cooked, which depending on what it is can take between 5 and 30 minutes. Root vegetables take longer than other vegetables, although the smaller you chop them the faster they'll cook. Green vegetables cook fast and are best added once the water is boiling.

## Steaming

This method of cooking uses the steam from boiling water to cook your food. You can either use a commercial, purpose-built steamer, or continuously boil water in a saucepan, keeping the lid tightly shut. It's essential that a pot doesn't boil dry, which is both dangerous and will damage the pan.

## One-pot cooking

This is a very popular method of cooking on camp. Not only is it relatively easy and tasty, it saves large amounts of washing up. You can cook casseroles, stews and dehydrated ready-meals this way.

## Roasting and grilling

Pieces of meat and whole or large pieces of vegetables can be roasted over a campfire on long skewers or spits, or placed on a metal grill supported over the fire on metal legs, large stones or logs. Brush the bars of the grill with oil before you start cooking, so that the food is less likely to stick to them.

## Pot roasting

This is a very slow but delicious way of cooking, best suited to a campfire unless you have plenty of stove fuel available. It's a way of cooking a large piece of meat without using an oven. A traditional 'Dutch oven' cooking pot (see page 156) is best, but any fairly large pot will do so long as it has a tight-fitting lid.

## Cooking in foil

Some foods can be wrapped in packets made from double layers of aluminium foil and placed directly on the hot embers of a campfire to cook. This method works best with foods such as sausages, burgers, fish, corn on the cob, onions, tomatoes, mushrooms, potatoes, apples, oranges and bananas. Large chunks of meat won't cook evenly. Cooking times vary depending on the food and the temperature of the embers, but sausages typically take about 30 minutes and potatoes about 40.

If you don't have any foil you can use layers of large leaves, such as cabbage, kale, 'greens' and romaine lettuce leaves, pegged closed with peeled and sharpened slivers of green wood. Always wash the leaves first. Never use rhubarb leaves, which are poisonous. Potatoes and onions can also be baked in their own skins.

## Cooking on hot stones

Scrub a flat stone and place it directly on top of the fire, supported on each side by smaller stones or logs to make a small altar. Once the stone heats through it can be used as a frying stone or griddle.

# FOOD STORAGE

While at camp ensure that you maintain the highest standard of cleanliness and food hygiene at all times. This is especially important when it comes to the storage of food.

Keeping food chilled is probably the most difficult challenge when outdoors. However, this can be met with careful menu planning and choosing ingredients that are safe to store. Make use of cool boxes, portable refrigerators and buy perishable items just before use.

High-risk foods are those generally intended to be consumed without any further cooking, which would destroy harmful bacteria. These include cooked meats and meat products, egg products and dairy foods; these should always be kept separate from raw food. Store raw meat, poultry, fish and vegetables in separate cool boxes. Make sure you have enough ice packs for this purpose and always check to see if the site has the facility to freeze these for you.

Take meat items frozen so that they can defrost slowly in a cool box. It is better to use long life milk or cream than fresh when camping, unless you can get regular fresh supplies. Treat as fresh once opened.

The risk of contracting an illness from canned foods is very small, but reject any cans that are badly dented, seam damaged, holed or rusty. When at camp, wipe the lids of cans before opening with a cloth dampened with antibacterial spray.

## Storage checklist:

- Keep food covered wherever possible.
- Do not use damaged or dirty equipment.
- Handle food as little as possible. Use tongs or similar if possible rather than hands.
- Insects, animals and birds must be prevented from entering or living in food preparation or storage areas. Remember squirrels are also pests and are very clever. Keep all packet foods in lidded containers; squirrels can, however, chew through plastic.
- When at camp the easiest way to avoid pest problems is not to leave any food or rubbish where it may attract them.
- Do not allow dried foods to become moist, as this will encourage the growth of bacteria and moulds.
- Put vegetables, salad and fruit in a cool box or lidded container.

# BACKWOODS COOKING

Backwoods cooking is the art of cooking without using traditional pots and pans, but using 'natural utensils' instead. It's an ideal activity for camp, where you have open fires and an abundance of wood.

## Getting started

The cooking techniques that can be used include roasting using a spit or on a stick kebab-style, baking in leaves or wet newspapers, baking one food inside another, and frying using a simple frying pan made out of silver foil and a pliable twig.

## Spud eggs

Cut the top off a potato and hollow it out. Crack an egg into it, replace the lid and wrap the potato in two layers of foil. Place the parcel in hot embers for 40 minutes. It's a good idea to check your potato after half an hour to ensure it isn't overcooked. Take care when unwrapping.

## Kebabs

Peel the bark from a long 'green' (ie living) stick and push a mixture of chopped sausages, onions, mushrooms, peppers and tomatoes on to it. Cook over hot embers until the sausage pieces are cooked right through. Take great care in choosing the wood both for your fire and skewers to ensure a pleasant taste and to avoid anything that's potentially harmful. Please see warning box below.

## Warning!

Make sure you never to use laurel, yew or horse chestnut wood when making toasting forks or skewers, as they're toxic. Ensure that the wood you burn to cook your food is also non-toxic. Cedar and pine are also best avoided as the smoke can give the food an unpleasant taste while fir and spruce are covered in an unappetising sticky resin.

## Chocolate banana

Slice an unpeeled banana in half lengthways and push chocolate buttons inside. Close it up, wrap in two layers of foil and cook in hot embers for up to 15 minutes. Be careful when unwrapping as the contents will be very hot and dispose of the foil responsibly as it could be harmful to wildlife.

## Twists or dampers

Mix self-raising flour, water, milk and an egg (or just plain flour, water and vegetable oil) to make a thick dough. Roll into a 'snake' and wrap it around a green stick (see above). Toast over embers until lightly browned and serve with butter and jam.

# BACKWOODS COOKING IDEAS

## Baked apple

Cut out the core of an apple, place the apple on foil and fill the hole with raisins, sultanas, sugar and, if desired, chocolate. Wrap in two layers of foil and cook in hot embers for 20 minutes or so. Eat with care, as the sugar gets very hot!

## Baked fish

Clean and gut your fish thoroughly beforehand. Wrap it in newspapers, wet thoroughly and place on the embers. Turn the fish several times at intervals of about 3–4 minutes until the newspaper is dried, and in about 15 minutes it's done.

## Campfire sausage rolls

Cook sausages in the normal way, ie on a stick or in a pan. Mix flour and water with a pinch of salt to make a dough (twists). Wrap the dough around the sausage, put on a stick and turn slowly over a campfire until light brown. Hey presto – sausage rolls!

## Sausage (or any meat) casserole

Wrap sausages (or finely chopped beef/chicken), chopped onion and any choice of other vegetables in cabbage leaves, seal with one layer of foil and put into embers for around 30 minutes.

## Chocolate porridge

To make a great breakfast using only one pan that you don't have to wash up, first boil a pan of water. Put half a hot chocolate sachet into a mug and an instant porridge sachet into a bowl. Use the boiling water to make up the hot chocolate in the mug and then pour it over the porridge; the result – chocolate porridge!

Put the rest of the hot chocolate sachet into the (now empty) mug, fill it up with most of the rest of the boiled water and drink it as a warming energiser to wash down the porridge. With the small bit of saved boiled water swill out the empty mug and bowl. It's perfect for lightweight expeditions, as it's quick and weighs almost nothing.

# DUTCH OVEN
# COOKING

If you'd prefer to cook with an oven rather than over a campfire, there are several alternatives. The Dutch oven is the simplest option and is able to do most of the things you can do with your oven at home. Plus it's much easier to carry!

## Go Dutch

Cast-iron Dutch ovens have been used for centuries for cooking outdoors, from the prairies of the American Mid-West and the Australian outback to the South African veldt and the Caribbean. The reason they're so popular is that they're extremely versatile and can be used for frying, baking, roasting, stewing and just about everything else.

## Buying and seasoning a Dutch oven

For maximum versatility buy one with legs, a bail arm and a recessed lid. Don't go for enamelled or aluminium Dutch ovens. Check that the casting is even all over, that the pot doesn't tilt when held by the bail arm, and that the lid makes a good seal.

Season the oven even if it's described as pre-seasoned. To do this, heat it and carefully wipe it inside and out with vegetable oil on a kitchen towel. Repeat this process several times to build up a thick, blackened coating.

## Using a Dutch oven

Dutch ovens can be used inside kitchen ovens, on gas and electric hobs, on barbeques and on campfires. However, don't heat an empty one over a direct flame or embers. Also, don't put hot or cold liquids into a hot Dutch oven.

A Dutch oven stays hot for a long while after being removed from the heat, meaning that the contents carry on cooking. So always remove it from the heat early enough to allow for this (and always wear thick gloves to handle it!). This is perfect for cooking rice – simply take

the oven off the heat when the rice is just done and it'll continue to cook and absorb all the water, meaning you don't need to drain.

To bake bread and cakes, use a baking tin resting on a couple of stones inside the oven, or even use the lid of a smaller Dutch oven.

For baking or roasting stand the Dutch oven on embers or coals and put more coals on the lid. Stack two or more Dutch ovens on top of each other to cook several courses at once. The embers on the lid of the lower pot will heat the bottom of the pot above it. Buy or make a lid lifter that enables you to remove a lid covered in embers without tipping them into your pot.

An upside-down Dutch oven lid can be used as a frying pan, skillet or hot plate for frying. This is also perfect for cooking popcorn!

When cooking sweet, sticky puddings some people line their Dutch ovens with tin foil to save washing up.

## Maintaining a Dutch oven

Always use wood or plastic utensils to avoid scratching, and never wash it with soapy water, which will remove its non-stick seasoning and will taint the taste of anything you cook in it afterwards. Simply wash it in hot water. Scrape any burnt-on bits with a wooden or plastic spatula or a washing-up sponge. If the burnt-on bits are really stubborn put the pot of water back on the heat and boil for a while.

Once it's clean, dry the oven over a gentle heat, then when it's dry wipe it over with a thin layer of oil.

If the Dutch oven is repeatedly used for boiling you may need to re-season it periodically. When storing it for long periods remove excess oil and leave the lid slightly open to allow air to circulate.

# MAKE A METAL BOX OVEN

This is a great way to make from scratch an oven that costs next to nothing. All you need is a well-cleaned biscuit or chocolate tin. If you're catering for larger numbers you could upgrade to an oil drum or similar, provided it's entirely cleaned.

**1** Dig a hole in a bank of earth or dig a trench. Make sure you get the landowner's permission first!

**2** Put the tin in the hole or over the trench.

**3** Light a fire beneath the tin and pile clay or earth around the oven on two sides. Clear away any loose stones or flint that may explode.

**4** Use the lid of the tin or a suitable metal sheet as the oven door. Insert a grid in the oven to provide a shelf so that the food isn't too close to the fire.

**5** Make a chimney at the back from tins, or a metal or clay drainpipe, and pile the earth around it.

# PROJECT: PONNACED TROUT

This is an ancient way of cooking and there's hardly a bushcraft school that doesn't use this technique on one course or another. It takes very little in the way of equipment and works really well.

**Difficulty**   **Total time** 30 minutes

## How to gut fish

The one in the pictures is shop-bought and ready-gutted, but should you have a fish with its innards still in place you need to carefully cut from the anus of the fish to the start of its tail and then back to the head. The blade mustn't go too deep or you risk nicking the internal organs and spoiling the fish. A good depth guide is to place your index finger on the back of the blade near the tip to prevent this happening. When doing this (and during all preparation stages) care must be taken to keep your fingers away from the cutting edge, as the trout is a slippery fish.

The next step is to make a cut all the way round the body at the head and tail, as shown in the pictures. Be sure to cut down to, but not through, the spine at the top. Now comes the slightly fiddly bit. Hold the trout upside-down, and with the other hand get your thumb gently between the top of the head and spine, and gently lever the spine away from the flesh, making sure that you carefully work under all the bones too. If you're dextrous you should end up with the head and tail still attached to the spine but separated from a nice neat butterflied trout.

## Cleaning fish

If you catch a fish it won't have been cleaned and gutted for you – you'll have to do this yourself.

It isn't always necessary to scale a fish, but if the scales are large use a knife to scrape from tail to head to remove them. Cut open the belly of the fish from its anus to its throat. Scoop out all the entrails.

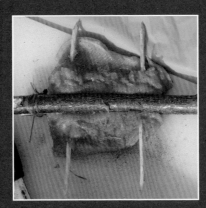

**1** You'll need to make a frame to hold your fish over the fire. Fresh hazel is the wood of choice and has been used here, because it's usually straight, is non-toxic, won't burn and generally splits well. Remember, don't use toxic species such as yew, laurel and holly.

**3** All that remains is to get the trout secured in the split stick. Gently pull the batoned split apart just enough to lower the skewered trout into it. Once it's in and lying flat, tie the split together at the top with wet string or fresh nettle cordage (this is why the split needs to be a little longer than the trout).

**5** The flesh can be cooked without anything on it, with a little salt and pepper, or a shop-bought spice mix if desired. The cooking time largely depends on the size of the fish and the embers you have, but may only be a few minutes. Adding a few fresh apple twigs to the embers will add an appealing smoky flavour.

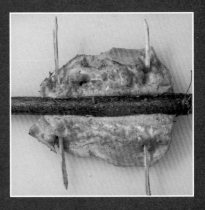

**2** You'll need two thin lengths of hazel to skewer through the flesh once you've pierced four well-spaced holes, and a length of hazel typically a little smaller than the diameter of a 10p coin and about 60cm in length. Make one end of this length into a point, and carefully baton or saw the other end to the length of the trout plus about 2.5cm. Have some spares ready in case the batoning goes wrong!

**4** To secure the hazel near the fire use a stick with a similar diameter – perhaps an offcut from the hazel – to make a hole in the ground with a slight lean towards the fire of no more than say 20° off vertical (because you don't want it too upright that it doesn't cook, and equally don't want it burning or falling into the fire). All the wood preparation and the hole can be done before preparing the fish but was done in this sequence here in order to show the process stage by stage.

**6** Several of these trout cooking together make for a great sight and aroma. Bacon, mackerel and salmon can all be cooked in a similar way.

# COUNTRYSIDE FORAGING

Wild food is far superior in flavour and nutritional content than shop-bought, cultivated and farmed food (plus it's free). Speak to locals about the best places to look and be especially aware of which plants and berries aren't safe to eat.

## Wild food

You'll have heard such phrases as 'nature's larder' and 'food for free', but is it really possible to head out to the beach or countryside with an empty basket and return with delicious things to eat? With the right knowledge of where to look and the right equipment, it's still possible. What's more, there are a huge number of ways to cook and prepare your food outdoors without the need of a kitchen or a complete set of utensils. Remember that the following is only an introduction to countryside foraging.

## Edible berries and nuts

If you're planning to gather wild berries, you should exercise extreme caution: there are no hard or fast rules regarding which are edible and which are poisonous. It's always best to check with an expert first. If you're in any doubt whatsoever, don't eat them – some are extremely toxic. However, the following five are all safe, if not necessarily satisfying!

### Rosehip

Rosehips are commonly oval and red. They're a source of vitamin C and have an acidic, slightly sweet taste.

### Hawthorn

The C. monogyna is the most common hawthorn. The red fruits have a large stone surrounded by a creamy-white flesh that's very slightly sweet, but frequently kicks in with a nasty aftertaste. The berries can be used in conserves and even wine can be made.

### Blackberry

Perhaps the tastiest berry freely available is the blackberry. Technically an aggregate fruit rather than a berry (it's made up of small fleshy segments called druplets), it comes into season in September and a myth says it should not be picked after 11 October (old Michaelmas). It's reputed to have excellent heath benefits: it is an antioxidant as well as a source of Vitimin C and folic acid.

### Rowan

The orange-red berries are bright and high in vitamin C – better made into a jelly for savoury dishes than eaten raw.

### Elder

Elderberries aren't to everyone's liking and can vary in bitterness. Although high in vitamin C they won't make a staple food.

### Sloe

Famous as the second most important ingredient in sloe gin, these blue/black berries are the fruit of the blackthorn shrub or tree. They're generally too tart to be eaten raw, but can be used in sloe and apple jam.

## Nuts

When it comes to hedgerow foraging in the UK you're generally on much safer ground with nuts. Sweet chestnuts, hazelnuts and walnuts are all safe to eat, though none of them are as widespread as they once were. These can all be eaten raw, but they taste better when roasted. Always get permission to collect them, since walnut trees in particular are only likely to be found on private land. Though they're commonplace, acorns should never be eaten raw – they require special preparation before they're edible.

## Wild garlic

Many flavourings are available when you cook in the wild. However, there's one in particular that many people smell but don't identify; this is wild garlic, also known as ramsons.

Not only can its bulbs be used in the later stages, but as they grow during May and June the root can be washed and chopped and added to salads, pasta or casseroles to add a strong, onion-type flavouring. Also the flowers can be chopped and added as a sweet variant to soups. The leaves can be made into pesto for mixing in with pasta, or simply included in salads as an extra variant with other leaves.

Make sure that wild garlic is washed well and that the utensils used for its preparation are kept separate so that the flavours aren't transferred to any other food that's being prepared.

# NETTLE TEA

You can make a drink from almost any edible plant, but there's one that's incredibly abundant in the wild and grows almost anywhere: urtica dioica, otherwise known as the stinging nettle.

Stinging nettles are relatively easy to harvest if you know how. If you look carefully at a nettle you'll see little spines or hairs on the leaves and stem; these are the things that sting when you brush up against them. However, if you're quick and squeeze it really tight you'll just bend these over and hopefully won't get stung. Make sure you grab the bottom of the nettle, as there are fewer spines down there! Better still, use gloves.

## Recipe

- Put your kettle on and boil some water.
- When you have your hot water, strip the nettle leaves from the stem and place them in a bowl or a pan. Rinse them with cold water to ensure that they're clean.
- Sieve the nettles from the pan/bowl and place them in your mug.
- Pour the hot water on the nettle leaves. This neutralises the chemicals used for stinging, allowing them to be consumed.
- Leave the tea to brew for 10–15 minutes, not just to allow the flavour to come out but to let the water cool for drinking.

Nettle tea tastes much like green tea. It has a fresh leafy flavour but is also quite bitter.

Now you have a choice: you can either drink it as it is or add lemon. This not only enhances the flavour of the nettles but also sweetens it. Adding lemon may also change the colour of the tea – this is normal.

# COASTAL FORAGING

If you prefer your free food a little more salty then why not try some coastal foraging? Not only is the backdrop suitably inspiring but you will discover a whole new world of delicious, unfamiliar delicacies.

## On the seashore

As the sun rises over a sleepy beach, the reflections of shimmering slender plants can be seen dancing in the shallows. As the tide recedes a wealth of plant life and shellfish can be found patiently clinging to the rocks. Seaweed and shellfish – Neptune's jewels – are highly nutritious, versatile and easily accessible. Together with fishing from the beach and the fish you may catch, a wide range of delicious plants can be found growing along the seashore, including many familiar, if now distant, relatives of the vegetables on offer from your local supermarket.

## Warning

If you get into difficulties for any reason and are unsure of your ability to make your way back safely, don't delay – phone 999 and ask for the coastguard. Remain calm, speak slowly and clearly. Help will arrive! Ensure that you check tide times before you set out and that you familiarise yourself with local safety procedures and any known local hazards.

## What to take

- Mobile phone (check for a good signal)
- Bucket (or basket) with handle
- Small tub
- Net bag or old onion sack
- Foraging or walking stick (also helps for stability on the rocks)
- Local tidal and weather information
- Torch or head lamp
- Waterproof clothing
- Watch
- Folding knife
- Compass

## Foraging essentials

Coastal foraging is best done in pairs for safety reasons, as exposed rocks and gullies can be covered with various seaweeds making them slippery at the best of times, and lethally so when wet. Caution should always be taken when out on exposed rocks, headlands and especially long surf beaches. A good prior understanding of the local area and its tidal and weather conditions is a must.

If you're unsure of the tide times wait until high tide and follow the falling tide out. You'll then have approximately six hours until it changes direction and starts to flood back in.

Never push your luck in search of a meal, or venture too far beyond the tidal limits, or walk along stretches of beach that are backed by steep cliffs. This could be life-threatening, as you can quickly become cut off from your route back. Sudden changes in wind and weather can affect the height of the tide in mere moments. Leave yourself plenty of time to make your way back in good daylight.

Always let somebody know where you're off to and what time you expect to return, especially if foraging alone. The local harbour master or coast guard can be contacted if you're unsure of your destination's suitability to forage both safely and responsibly. They may also be able to help with information regarding weather and local tidal conditions.

Some areas of the coast may have restrictions regarding access, especially in military and conservation areas. Always check with the relevant local authorities if you're unsure. Beaches and coastlines where restrictions apply are normally signposted accordingly.

It's a good idea to get a tide table in advance for the area you're visiting, to help you plan your foraging in relation to the best tide times. The RNLI produce good tide tables that are available from their shops. Also, most angling centres and shops have them, or you can look online. If you've checked the local tide times and weather conditions and they're favourable, the most likely danger is slipping or falling and sustaining an injury.

## Crabbing

A true family activity, crabbing requires an element of skill, a little knowledge and lots of patience. There are, however, some proven hints and tips that will help you hook a crab. The best kinds of bait are meat-based – so chicken, cat food and bacon all work well, but make sure that the bait makes it all the way down to the sea bed. If it

is floating above it, or caught in seaweed, then you won't catch a thing. Once you have a 'bite', reel it in very slowly to avoid the crab jumping off. Crabs should be stored in a bucket half-filled with seawater and shaded from the sun. You must release them back into the water (and not from a great height) after your crabbing session.

# SEA VEGGIES

Here are just some of the treats in store for the intrepid coastal forager.

### Sea kale

Easily recognised in summer from its white flowers, sea kale is an indigenous vegetable found mostly on England's south coast.

### Sea beet

Related to beetroot and sugar beet, and recognised by spiky green flowers (which appear around July), red/green stems and oval leaves.

### Sugar wrack

With a slippery yellowish leaf, the sugar wrack is more appetising than it looks. It is often found hanging off rocks and harbour walls.

### Wild carrot

Wild carrot is recognisable from its small white flowers. The roots are edible and best eaten when young as they become woody with age.

### Sea parsnip

A prickly herb, identified by its yellowish-white flowers, it makes an unusual addition to any dinner plate.

### Dulse

An edible red algae, dulse is best harvested in the summer (July to September) and can be found on the sea shore on rocks at low tide.

# FIRST AID AND SURVIVAL

The outdoors is an unpredictable place. It's therefore vital you are ready for any situation that might develop which might result in injury or threat to life. There are a number of techniques, skills and procedures that should be learned to ensure you're well prepared for an emergency situation. No textbook is a substitute for attending a first aid training course, but this section will give you a good grasp of the basics — with the right attitude and preparation, anyone can give first aid.

# WHAT IS FIRST AID?

Any outdoor activity can potentially result in an accident, so it's essential that you have a basic understanding of first aid. A great deal of this is common sense. For example, if someone's bleeding then the first thing that you need to do is to stop the bleeding.

## Reassuring patients

Being able to talk to people is the first step in reassuring someone who's injured and possibly anxious, worried and confused. Practise talking to someone in a quiet but confident way. A simple reassuring hand on the shoulder can go a long way, as does checking the hand to see if it's cold.

Find out the casualty's name. Crouch down so you're at the same height as them. Talk in a manner that's kind and gentle but firm and direct to build trust and confidence between you. Whilst providing a bit of comfort this also calms people down, which will help you to get on with the job at hand.

If you feel pressured, take a few deep breaths and only take a decision when you're in a clear, calm state of mind. Always explain to the patient what actions you're planning to take. If you're treating children, and parents are present, involve the parents too and gain their trust and approval before you continue. Use simple language when talking to children.

Listen carefully to what the casualty is telling you, nodding and confirming verbally that you've understood them. Repeat and summarise what the patient has told you. Don't interrupt.

If a casualty refuses help or first aid, contact 999 and explain the situation; continue to monitor the situation. If you need to attend to another casualty, ensure someone stays with your patient; they should never be left alone.

Remember the following key points:
- Always remember to act calmly.
- Consider risks and needs.
- State who you are and what you'll do.
- Listen, learn and empathise.
- Manage and promote dignity, respect and privacy.
- Enable decision-making by providing relevant information and facilitating choice.
- Prioritise contact with other people who can help.
- Utilise available support and seek additional help where it's required and wanted.

## Managing an incident

Look for possible risks and identify what resources are available in terms of people, supplies and equipment. Use your common sense judgement to assess the risks and formulate an appropriate response. Determine what dangers are present. If the casualty is threatened by further injury, do what you can to make the area safer – for example, by switching off the ignition of a car. Only move a casualty as a very last resort.

## Delegate tasks

In the case of a large incident you'll need to ask other people to help. Delegate the following tasks:

- Control traffic.
- Call 999.
- Obtain equipment or supplies.
- Protect privacy.
- Transport the casualty.
- Take care of personal belongings.
- Contact next of kin.

## Preventing cross-infection

- Wherever possible, wash your hands and wear a pair of gloves if they are available.
- Cover cuts and grazes on your own hands with waterproof dressings.
- Don't sneeze, cough or breathe near a wound while it's being treated.
- Don't touch a wound or any part of a dressing that will come into contact with a wound.
- Dispose of any waste products carefully.

## Teaching yourself

When practising first aid you'll need someone to practise on and some dressings and bandages with which to practise. Items that are out of date or no longer sterile are ideal for this purpose.

Before attempting any first aid you should familiarise yourself with the contents of a first aid kit and how to use them. Practise opening and putting on plasters, bandages and dressings without touching the medicated pad or the part that will be in contact with the injury.

# FIRST AID KITS

It is important to familiarise yourself with the contents of a first aid kit and how to use them

A first aid kit should always be available and should contain the following items:

- Adhesive plasters of varying sizes
- Crepe bandages
- Sterile dressings
- Triangular bandage
- Adhesive tape
- Safety pins
- Tweezers
- Notebook and pencil

All dressings, plasters and bandages should be individually wrapped to ensure that they're sterile, and checked that they're 'in date'. All equipment should be kept in a dry, clean, airtight box that's clearly labelled and accessible.

## Health and hygiene

Practising good hygiene when in the outdoors goes a long way towards staying healthy. A large part of the fun of camping, or any activity outdoors, is being able to leave behind the daily routines of make-up, hairstyling and shaving. Staying hygienic, however, is really important, for the sake of both your own health and the environment in which you're staying. Camping or outdoor activities shouldn't necessarily mean roughing it, and the same basic personal hygiene should be practised as far as possible.

If you plan to use a natural water supply to wash, or will be disposing of used water into the environment, it's important to use biodegradable items which won't contaminate the local water supply. Possibly easier are wet wipes or baby wipes, which can be burnt after use or taken home. Antibacterial hand gel is really useful for keeping hands clean before eating or cooking.

When considering toileting, it's not really acceptable to just 'go in the woods' – again, consider the environmental impact, as well as other people using the area. If you need to urinate, choose a spot that's clear of vegetation yet secluded, and make sure it's not near a water supply. For defecating, a hole should ideally be dug and toilet paper burnt, not buried.

Finally, don't forget that strongly scented perfumes or cosmetics may attract mosquitoes or other flying insects, which are not only annoying but also carry disease.

# FIRST AID TREATMENT

We've teamed up with the British Red Cross to provide advice on first aid treatment. Learning first aid is easy. In fact, you'd be surprised at just how simple it is to pick up the basic knowledge. It only takes a few minutes to learn new skills that could make all the difference.

## Serious injuries

Always treat serious injuries first. There are three conditions that immediately threaten life:

- Breathing problems
- Heart problems
- Serious bleeding

When there's more than one injured person, go to the quiet one first. They may be unconscious and in need of immediate attention. Remember your own needs throughout!

In the following descriptions of treatments, please note that a baby is someone aged up to one year old, and a child is someone aged between one and puberty.

## Unconscious adults

To check if the person is conscious, try to get a response by gently shaking their shoulders and calling their name. If there's no response:

**1** Open the airway by placing one hand on their forehead and gently tilting the head back and lifting the chin. Remove any visible obstructions from the mouth and nose.

**2** Check breathing by looking, listening and feeling for breathing on your cheek for up to 10 seconds.

### Resuscitation (adult)

If the person isn't breathing normally, you must call an ambulance then start cardio-pulmonary resuscitation (CPR), which is a combination of chest compressions and rescue breaths:

**1** Place your hands on the centre of their chest and, with the heel of your hand, press down (5–6cm) at a rate of 100–120 a minute. After every 30 chest compressions give two breaths.

**2** Open the airway, place one hand on the forehead and gently tilt the head back and lift the chin. Pinch the person's nose. Place your mouth over their mouth and – by blowing steadily – attempt two rescue breaths, each lasting one second.

**3** Continue with cycles of 30 chest compressions and two rescue breaths until emergency help arrives or the person shows signs of regaining consciousness, such as coughing, opening their eyes, speaking or moving purposefully and starting to breathe normally. If you're unable or unwilling to give rescue breaths, you can give chest compressions alone.

If they're breathing normally:

- Treat any life-threatening injuries and put them on their side with their head tilted back.
- Check breathing.
- Call 999 and monitor the casualty's condition until help arrives.

Photo ©Layton Thompson/British Red Cross

Photo ©Layton Thompson/British Red Cross

### Resuscitation (child)

If a child isn't breathing give one minute of CPR then call 999 for an ambulance. If another person is present ask them to call an ambulance straight away.

**1** Open the airway: place one hand on the forehead, gently tilt the head back and lift the chin.

**2** Remove any visible obstructions from the mouth and nose.

**3** Pinch the child's nose. Place your mouth over the child's mouth and attempt five initial rescue breaths.

**4** Place your hands on the centre of their chest and, with the heel of your hand, press down one-third of the depth of the chest using one or two hands depending on the size of the child and your own size, at a rate of 100–120 per minute. After every 30 chest compressions give two breaths.

**5** Continue with cycles of 30 chest compressions and two rescue breaths until help arrives or the child shows signs of regaining consciousness, such as coughing, opening their eyes, speaking or moving purposefully and starting to breathe normally.

If you're unable or unwilling to give rescue breaths, you can give chest compressions alone.

If they're breathing normally:

- Treat any life-threatening injuries and put them on their side with their head tilted back.
- Check breathing.
- Call 999 and monitor the casualty's condition until help arrives.

Photo ©Alex Rumford/British Red Cross

Photo ©Alex Rumford/British Red Cross

## Bleeding

In some ways the human body is like a central heating system: the heart is a pump, and the veins and arteries are the pipes. If a pipe is punctured, then water leaks out. The body is the same – if the skin is punctured, then blood will leak out. The solution to both problems is to plug the hole. However, additional precautions are needed with the body.

Any break in the skin, however small, can allow bacteria to enter the body. If allowed to settle in a wound these micro-organisms – carried, for example, by flies or unwashed hands – will grow and cause infection.

When dealing with simple cuts and grazes you should take the following steps to prevent this:

- Sit the casualty down and temporarily protect the wound by covering it with a clean piece of gauze.
- Wash your hands.
- Rinse the wound under cold running water until it's clean unless a clot has started to form and you feel it would be better to leave it, as washing it would cause it to start bleeding again.
- In the case of grazes, where there's more chance of dirt and germs being present, further clean the wound using wet cotton wool. Always clean from the centre of the wound outwards.
- Dry the area around the wound and place a dressing over it. Never dress a wound with cotton wool or anything fluffy.

### Nosebleeds

**1** Ensure the person is sitting down. Advise them to tilt their head forwards to allow the blood to drain from the nostrils.

**2** Ask the person to pinch together the end of their nose and breathe through their mouth.

**3** After 10 minutes, release the pressure. If the bleeding hasn't stopped, reapply the pressure for up to two further periods of 10 minutes.

**4** If bleeding still continues, seek medical advice.

Discourage the casualty from coughing or swallowing until the bleeding stops. It may be helpful to place a bowl on the floor to catch any dripping blood. Also advise them not to touch or blow their nose for several hours after bleeding has stopped. This will prevent disturbing the clot and prevent the bleeding from restarting.

If bleeding from the nose follows a blow to the head this could indicate a fracture of the skull and the casualty should receive urgent professional medical help.

### Severe bleeding

Blood loss can be serious and should be treated as quickly as possible. Your main aim is to stem the flow of blood. If you have disposable gloves available, use them – it's important to reduce the risk of cross-infection at all times.

**1** Press on the wound with your hand, ideally over a clean pad, and secure with a bandage.

**2** Raise the wound above the level of the heart.

### Embedded object in wound

If you suspect there's something embedded, take care not to press on the object. Instead press firmly on either side of it and build up padding around it before bandaging, to avoid putting pressure on the object itself. Get the person to hospital as quickly as possible.

## Choking adult or child

**1** Give up to five back blows between his shoulder blades with the heel of your hand.

**2** Check his mouth quickly after each one and remove any obvious obstruction. If the obstruction is still present:

**3** Give up to five abdominal thrusts. Place your clenched fist above his navel, cover your fist with your other hand and pull sharply inwards and upwards. Check his mouth quickly after each thrust.

**4** If the obstruction doesn't clear after three cycles of back blows and abdominal thrusts dial 999 for an ambulance.

**5** Continue until help arrives and resuscitate if necessary.

**For information on the correct response for baby choking and baby resuscitation, please see www.redcross.org.uk/everydayfirstaid**

## Burns and scalds

Burns (caused by dry heat) and scalds (caused by wet heat) are among the most common injuries requiring emergency treatment in the UK.

**1** Cool the burn as quickly as possible by placing the affected area under cold running water for at least 10 minutes or until pain is relieved.

**2** Cover the burn with cling film placed lengthways over the injury. A clean plastic bag is ideal to cover a hand or foot. Alternatively use a sterile dressing.

**3** Always seek medical advice if the casualty is a baby or child.

Watch out for signs and symptoms of shock (see below). If present, seek professional medical help.

Photo ©Alex Rumford/British Red Cross

## Shock

The most likely cause of shock is serious bleeding or a severe burn or scald. This life-threatening condition occurs when vital organs don't get enough oxygen due to reduced blood circulation. These injuries must be treated immediately. There could be internal bleeding if there are signs of shock and no visible injury. Early signs of shock are:

- Pale, cold and sweaty skin, tinged with grey.
- Rapid pulse becoming weaker.
- Shallow, fast breathing.

As it develops you'll notice:

- Restlessness.
- Yawning and sighing.
- Severe thirst.

First treat any obvious injuries. Lie the person on a blanket to keep them warm. Reassure them. Raise and support the legs above the level of their heart and loosen tight clothing. Dial 999 for an ambulance and resuscitate if necessary. Don't give anything to eat or drink, as they may later need a general anaesthetic in hospital.

Many people confuse shock with being psychologically shocked. The first is a physical response associated with an injury or condition (which can be life-threatening if not appropriately treated), the second is an emotional response.

## Strains and sprains

A strain is a pulled or torn muscle, while a sprain results from overstretching the supporting ligaments around a joint. Both should be treated initially by the 'RICE' procedure:

**R** – rest the injured part.
**I** – apply ice or a cold compress.
**C** – comfortably support the injury.
**E** – elevate the injured part.

An ideal compress is a packet of frozen veg wrapped in cloth – a T-shirt, towel or whatever you have to hand can be used.

This treatment may be sufficient to relieve the symptoms, but if you don't know how severe the injury is treat it as a fracture and seek medical advice.

## Allergic reaction

An allergy is an abnormal reaction of the body's defence system to a normally harmless trigger substance. Common triggers include pollen dust, nuts, shellfish, eggs, wasp and bee stings, latex and certain medications. People who know they suffer from this condition often carry medication in the form of an auto-injector (epi-pen). Symptoms of an allergic reaction include:

- Swelling and itching, especially in the area that came into contact with the trigger – if food, for instance, the swelling will be round the mouth and throat.
- Blotchy red skin or itchy rash spreading over the body.
- Swollen, itchy eyes.
- Swelling in the throat, difficulty breathing or wheezing.
- Dizziness, anxiety and apprehension.
- Stomach cramps, vomiting or diarrhoea.
- Sudden drop in blood pressure leading to unconsciousness.

If someone suffers from a severe reaction, known as anaphylaxis, or anaphylactic shock:

**1** Dial 999 for an ambulance.

**2** If the person is conscious and has medication such as an auto-injector, help them to use it. If they're unable to do it themselves, hold the auto-injector in your fist, pull off the safety cap and press the tip against their thigh through their clothing. This will automatically inject the person with the drug.

**3** Help them to sit comfortably.

Be prepared to resuscitate the person if necessary.

Photo ©Alex Rumford/British Red Cross

## Broken bones

The common causes of broken bones are direct force, such as a kick; indirect force, for example a fall on an outstretched hand can break the collarbone; and twisting force – for example, a foot stuck in a hole can break the ankle. The signs and symptoms of a broken bone are:

- Pain.
- Bruising and swelling.
- Difficulty with movement.
- Deformity.
- Shock.

It can be difficult to distinguish between bone, joint and muscle injuries, so if in doubt treat the injury as a broken bone. Your main aim is to prevent further injury by keeping the casualty still, and then to get them to hospital.

**1** Encourage the person to keep still.

**2** Steadily support the injured limb.

**3** If the fracture is open, where covering skin is broken or bone is sticking through the skin, cover it with a sterile dressing.

**4** Treat any shock.

## Sling for an injured arm

Making a sling is easy. All you need is a piece of clean cloth measuring about 1.5m by 0.9m, folded to form a triangular bandage.

**1** If necessary support the injured arm with a piece of wood, stiff card or rolled paper.

**2** Gently slide the triangular bandage underneath the arm, keeping the hands free.

**3** Lift the bottom corner and knot around the neck. Fold the third corner over the elbow and pin in place.

If you don't have a large enough piece of cloth, and don't have a triangular bandage in your first aid kit, use a jumper and knot the sleeves together.

## Hypothermia

Hypothermia occurs when the body temperature drops below 35°C (95°F).

Children are most at risk when they've been active outdoors for a long time in low temperatures, or have become wet (by falling into cold water, for example). Symptoms include:

- Shivering.
- Cold, pale, dry skin.
- Listlessness or confusion.
- Failing consciousness.
- Slow, shallow breathing.
- Weakening pulse.

### Action to take

- Prevent further body heat loss.
- Warm the casualty.
- Get medical help.
- Dress the person warmly (including a hat) and cover with plenty of blankets.
- If possible give the person a warm (not hot) bath. Dry them quickly and wrap in warm towels or blankets.
- Give warm drinks.
- Give them high-energy foods such as chocolate.

## Heat exhaustion

This condition is caused by an abnormal loss of salt and water from the body through excessive sweating. It usually develops gradually and is more likely to affect people who aren't accustomed to hot and humid conditions, and those who are already ill. Signs and symptoms are:

- Cramp-like pains and/or headache.
- Pale, moist skin.
- Fast, weak pulse.
- Slightly raised temperature.

### Action to take

- Help the casualty to lie down in a cool place.
- Raise their legs to improve blood flow.
- Fan the casualty and cool them with water.
- Give them plenty of water or a non-fizzy drink to replace lost fluids.
- Call 999 for an ambulance.

## Sunburn

Move the patient out of the sunlight or cover their skin with light clothing. Ask them to take sips of cold water. Dab the damaged skin with cold water. Apply calamine or after-sun lotion.

## Dehydration

About three-quarters of our body is made up of water, which we constantly lose through breathing, sweating and urinating. If we don't replace this lost water our body will begin to dehydrate and eventually die. People can become dehydrated in any conditions simply by failing to sufficiently replace their natural fluid loss. Signs of dehydration include:

- Feeling thirsty.
- Dry mouth, eyes and lips.
- Lack of appetite.
- Impatience.
- Lethargy and nausea.
- Headache.
- Dizziness or light-headedness.
- Inability to walk.
- Delirium.

Photo ©Matthew Percival/British Red Cross

Someone suffering from dehydration should find a shady area to rest in, drink fluids slowly, keep cool and avoid sweating.

## Insect stings and bites

If you can see the sting, scrape it away carefully with your fingernail or credit card. Don't try to remove it with tweezers, because the sting may have a venom sac attached and you may squeeze more venom into the wound.

Apply an ice pack on the affected area to reduce pain and swelling. You can use a packet of frozen veg wrapped in cloth – a T-shirt, towel or whatever you have to hand.

Keep the injured part in a comfortable position, preferably raised, until the pain and swelling ease. If you're concerned about continued pain and swelling, get medical help.

If you're bitten by a tick, remove the tick using tweezers. Grasp its head as close to the person's skin as you can and pull the tick upwards, using steady, even pressure. Place the tick in a sealed plastic bag. The patient should seek medical advice and take the tick with them, as it may be needed for identification.

## Blisters

Blisters are an occupational hazard for outdoor adventurers. If one develops the most important thing to do is to keep the affected area clean, washing with plenty of clean water. Gently dry with a gauze pad, then attach a plaster, ensuring the pad of the plaster covers the whole blister. A blister pad is even better.

### Further information

Further information can be obtained from the British Red Cross and local first aid courses. To see first aid advice in action you can watch videos, check out frequently asked questions and test your skills at redcross.org.uk/everydayfirstaid

# IMPROVISED STRETCHER

There may be occasions when you'll need to transport a casualty who cannot walk and will need to improvise a stretcher. You'll need to use whatever you have to hand.

### Blanket

If you have some poles and a blanket (some foil emergency blankets are surprisingly strong) or a piece of material, such as a tent flysheet, you can make a stretcher. If you don't have long poles or Scout staves you can lash two walking poles together for each side (you can use shoe/boot laces from the casualty for the lashings).

Fold about a third of the blanket over one of the poles and then place the second pole on the folded part so that enough material can be folded back over the pole and be roughly in the middle where the casualty will lay. Then fold over the bottom piece of material.

Even if you don't have poles you can still make a stretcher. Place the casualty in the centre of the blanket/material and then roll the sides in towards the casualty. You can then carry the stretcher using the rolled up material as handles. You'll need four people to carry this type of stretcher.

### Coats and poles

If you don't have any suitable blankets or material you can also use two coats, fleeces or waterproofs. If possible turn the coat sleeves inside out and button or zip up the coat. Place the coats with their hems touching and thread the poles through the armholes, inside one coat and then through the inside sleeves and out through the armholes of the second coat. As before you can also lash together walking poles.

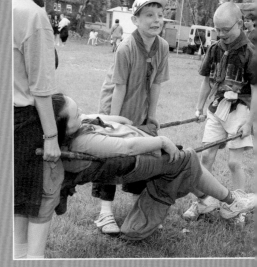

You can carry this type of improvised stretcher with two people but four are better.

### Rope stretcher

If you don't have any poles but do have some rope you can still make a crude stretcher. The rope needs to be long enough for about nine zigzags under the casualty, and you'll need five or six people. Lay the rope as a zigzag with each part being under the heavier parts of body – shoulders, chest, waist, buttocks, thighs, calves and ankles. You'll need a separate person to support the casualty's head. To make it more comfortable you can lay coats/clothing on the rope 'cradle'.

# SURVIVAL EQUIPMENT

When planning what to take on a serious expedition, examine the variety of specialist equipment that could save your life in an emergency. From water purification kits to windproof matches, this section describes a range of items you should consider.

### Personal locator beacon

This is vital to anyone who's venturing off the beaten track, especially in winter conditions, during skiing or on other alpine expeditions. It will enable the search party to find you more easily when time is likely to be a factor in your survival.

### Water purification kit

Fitted with a ceramic filter, these kits are nevertheless lightweight and highly portable. Screening out 99.9% of harmless bacteria, this is a lifesaver when your clean water supplies run out.

### Safety light stick

Simply bend until you hear the crack of the chemical being released. Each stick will provide emergency light for up to 12 hours (check the packet first, as the duration of light varies).

### Survival kit

Survival kits are usually packed in small tin containers, rather like the tins that old-fashioned travel sweets used to come in. However, you're unlikely to find them full of sherbet lemons. Instead, they contain an amazing assortment of gadgets that'll help keep you alive. This by no means exhaustive list includes a knife, snare wire, fishing kit, flint and striker, sewing kit, safety pins, wire saw, waterproof matches and plasters.

### Mirror and whistle

You don't need to spend a lot of money to stay safe; a simple mirror (or piece of metal with a highly polished surface) and whistle will greatly increase your chances of being found if stranded in the wild.

### Location marker dye

There are many products available that allow you to spread a fluorescent dye into the environment, such as in water or snow. These will again help you be spotted by search and rescue teams. The dye can be seen from as far as a mile away.

### Hammock and mosquito net

Investing in a good-quality hammock will mean a much better night's sleep. Not only does it save you from sleeping on cold, bumpy ground, but the net will also protect you from midges, mosquitoes and other creepy crawlies.

### Windproof matches

So you've heard of waterproof matches, but what about windproof? Used by members of the armed services across the world, they burn for over ten seconds and cannot be blown out, even if dropped in water!

### Flint and steel

Even if you forget everything else, you simply must have a failsafe way of lighting a fire. A good-quality flint and steel combination will provide over 2,000 sparks.

### Survival blanket

You'll be familiar with the metallic blankets you see marathon runners wear at the end of races. These survival blankets work on the same principle – trapping air and preventing heat loss. They offer excellent protection against hypothermia.

### Lightweight tarp

A tarp and rope is the quickest way to rig a shelter in the wild. It can be up in a matter of minutes and has the advantage of taking up very little room. You can also rig it above your hammock to provide a complete hotel room in the wild.

## Being seen

If an emergency should arise and you don't have a phone or phone signal, and cannot make further progress, it's best to remain where you are and wait for your home contact to realise that something's wrong and alert the emergency services. Create a temporary shelter if you can, erect your tent if you have one, and at the very least get into a bothy bag or wrap yourself in your survival blanket. Make any injured members of your party as comfortable as possible. Your next priority is to be seen, especially from the air, so use any brightly coloured or reflective materials you may have, such as mirrors, clothing and metallic objects.

# SURVIVAL PRIORITIES

There's an established sequence of steps to follow if you find yourself in a survival situation. This will ensure the safety of yourself and others.

## Shelter

A good shelter will help you stay dry as well as protect you from the elements. This could either be one that's found naturally (such as a cave) or one that you build yourself (see page 62 on how to build an A-frame shelter). Sleep is essential to restore energy.

## Fire

Fire is vital, not just for warmth but for cooking, water purification and deterring pests, both large and small.

## Water

You can only survive three to four days without water, so you must find a clean, reliable source. If water is very limited, do strenuous tasks at night to avoid excessive fluid loss. Breathing through the nose and not eating too much are other ways to conserve the body's water.

## First aid

Once you've looked after shelter, fire and water, it's time to treat non-life-threatening medical conditions.

## Food

Whether fishing, hunting or gathering fruit, nuts and other edible vegetation, it's important to know how to live off the land, at least for a short time. Refer to pages 160–163 for advice on food and foraging.

## Rescue

Knowledge of signalling (see pages 100–103) will be invaluable when alerting others to your presence.

# EXTREME SURVIVAL

No matter how good your planning, things can sometimes still go wrong. Freak weather conditions, a landslide or forest fire can quickly develop into a life-threatening situation. Always hope for the best and prepare for the worst.

## How to survive an avalanche

Avalanches claim the lives of over 150 people each year worldwide. While rarely predictable, the best advice is to avoid known avalanche black spots and seek as much knowledge as possible about local weather conditions, which may result in a dangerous thaw of snow and ice. Otherwise, follow these steps to maximise your chances of survival.

### Jump up

Since many avalanches are caused by skiers and climbers themselves, the avalanche may begin right at your feet. Try to jump up from the point where the snow or ice shelf has separated.

### Move to the side

If you see an avalanche coming towards you, the advice is simple – get out of its way. Move to the side nearest you, and try and get as clear as possible. The main force of the avalanche is in the centre, so the further away you are from this the better.

### Stay upright

Being able to use your feet means you'll have a better chance of scrambling out of trouble. If you do lose your balance, drop your poles, rucksack or other equipment, as these may drag you further down.

## Inflatable backpacks

There are inflatable backpacks available that can be used in the event of being caught in an avalanche. They're currently rather expensive; however, like all new gadgets the price will eventually come down. Again, it all depends on where you do your adventuring. If your mountain travel is restricted to the Peak District you're unlikely to need one.

### Get a grip

Try and get hold of a fixed object such as a large rock or tree – the longer you can keep hold of this the better.

### Swim

It sounds preposterous, but the advice is to swim in the direction of the snow to stay on top of it (any stroke will do, but backstroke is said to be the best as it allows you to see objects coming towards you).

### Make a breathing space

As the avalanche slows, take a deep breath and cup your hands in front of your mouth to create an air pocket. Stay calm and await rescue.

## How to survive in snow

Getting lost in a blank, white wilderness can be terrifying. Without any identifying features even roads and rivers can be obscured, making navigation difficult. If you find yourself lost in snow it's essential you find shelter before nightfall. Here's how to make a tree-pit snow shelter:

- Find an evergreen tree with good overhanging branches to provide shelter.
- Around the trunk, dig out the snow down to a depth of approximately 1.2m.
- Lay evergreen branches over the top and on the floor of the shelter for cover and insulation.

## How to escape mud or quicksand

No matter how scared you are, try not to panic or make any sudden movements. If you're only up to your ankles or knees, try to step back, pulling your legs out one at a time. If you find yourself up to your waist, slowly lie back to distribute your weight evenly and try to float on your back. You can then pull your legs out one at a time. Once your legs are free, roll over, rather than crawl or walk out. If you cannot reach dry land, try and spread yourself out as wide as you can to distribute your weight further, and try to wriggle out by moving your body.

## How to stay afloat

In open water your chances of survival will be greatly increased if you have a flotation device. While you should, of course, always wear a lifejacket if taking part in any water activities, here's a way to prepare an improvised float for an emergency:

- Purchase a heavy-duty child's balloon.
- Store this inside a heavy-duty plastic shopping bag.
- Fold these together and secure with a strong rubber band.
- In the event of an emergency, blow up the balloon and leave this inside the bag. Holding the bag upside-down by its handles will keep you afloat.

## How to survive a forest fire

Fire spreads incredibly quickly and a fierce forest fire is almost impossible to outrun. Counter-intuitively, fire actually travels more quickly uphill than downhill, so head downhill if you can. Head for deciduous trees rather than evergreens, as they burn slowly. The most important thing to do, however, is get to a place where the fire cannot burn, such as a river or road.

If the fire has caught up with you on all sides, find or dig a ditch or trench. Climb in and make yourself as small as possible, covering yourself over with a coat or blanket, preferably soaked in water. Wait for the fire to pass over you, then escape upwind.

# A–Z OF OUTDOOR ADVENTURE

There are over 200 different activities to try in Scouting, from abseiling to zorbing, each with their own required levels of skill and expertise. Most can be tried inexpensively in Scouting or through a recognised provider without the need to invest in expensive kit.

### Abseiling

Abseiling is a form of descending from a height using a rope. This activity is usually undertaken on a rockface or a man-made structure.

### Aerial runway

An aerial runway is a rope slide that stretches between two fixed points, and is angled sufficiently to enable a pulley block to slide down its length using gravity as its only source of propulsion. The aim is to move a person from point A to point B, often over some kind of obstruction such as a ravine, piece of water, rough ground or similar. The 'rider' goes to the start point, is secured into the seat and then lets the pulley slide down the course of the runway until it reaches its finish point, where the 'rider' dismounts.

### Archery

Target archery is an internationally recognised sport which features in both the Commonwealth and Olympic Games. This is the most popular form of the sport where, as its name suggests, participants shoot at static targets in order to score points. The range from which people fire and the size of the target vary. A round consists of a number of 'ends' of arrows, ie the number of arrows that each archer shoots prior to the scores being recorded and the arrows collected. Ends normally consist of three arrows when shooting indoors, and six when outdoors.

### Canoeing

Open boats have been used for thousands of years by many different cultures, but it was native North Americans who pioneered the craft we recognise as canoes today, making them from wooden ribs and bark and using them to navigate the vast river networks of the continent. When European settlers arrived, early explorers used canoes to chart their New World. Today they're often known as 'Canadian canoes'.

### Canyoning

Canyoning is the activity of following a riverbed through a deep gorge, often with high mountain sides. This often includes climbing, swimming, abseiling and scrambling, depending upon the environment.

### Caving

Being a completely alien and unseen environment, caves have for generations been regarded by many as the domain of the sinister, and all those who participate in the activity looked upon as equally strange folks. Nothing could be further from the truth. Not only are caves some of the most beautiful places on Earth, they only show their beauty to those who explore their depths.

### Coasteering

Coasteering involves traversing the interface between sea and land on foot. It will take you scrambling over rocks, jumping from cliffs, swimming in the sea and getting washed by waves. You'll be scared and excited at the same time, and if all this doesn't push up your adrenaline levels it'll simply unwind you. Truly unforgettable!

### Crate climbing

This involes placing one crate on top of another, with the climber remaining standing on the topmost crate without dismounting at any time. The aim is to see how high you can get before the pile of crates topples over or the climber falls off. The climber will start by standing on top of one crate, which is placed on the ground. They then attempt to place another crate on top of the first and manoeuvre themselves to stand on top of it, and then further crates on top of that, and so on.

### Grass sledging

Grass sledging is the summer equivalent to the winter sport of tobogganing, the difference being that the participant travels down a grass slope whilst sitting on a sledge which uses small wheels in place of runners. It can be run as a timed event or, if more than one sledge is available, as a straight race to the finish line. The course is usually a straight line, as there's little a sledger can do to influence the direction of travel!

### Hang-gliding

Hang-glider pilots, suspended from their gliders by a special harness, launch from hills facing into the wind, from winches on flat ground, or by being towed aloft behind a microlight aircraft. The objective is to stay airborne in lifting currents of air and – for many – to undertake long cross-country flights. The UK record for distance currently stands at over 250km, and for altitude at an astonishing 16,000ft.

Circling up to cloudbase on a summer's day and setting course on a long cross-country flight over patchwork fields is one of the wonders of the modern world. Landing out after a long flight using only the natural power of the atmosphere and their accumulated knowledge of the sky gives a hang-glider pilot an unsurpassed feeling of accomplishment.

### Kayaking

Originally used by the Inuits for hunting and fishing, a kayak is propelled from a sitting position using a double-ended paddle. Most commonly these boats have enclosed decks (closed cockpit) and are designed for a single person, although you can get open-cockpit kayaks and kayaks for two or more people.

### Land yachting

Land yachting is an environmentally-friendly activity which, while being highly enjoyable, produces no noise, pollution or damage to its surroundings. A land yacht is a fast, wind-propelled craft which operates on land. It looks like a long, thin, three-wheeled buggy with enough room for one person to sit inside and a sail attached to make it move. Average land yachts reach speeds of about 50mph, while the world record is 116mph.

### Mountain biking

Mountain biking involves travelling by mountain cycle away from roads on difficult and challenging terrain.

### Orienteering

Providing the suspense and excitement of a treasure hunt, orienteering is an adventurous activity for people of all ages, fitness and skill levels. Participants navigate their way between control points marked on a specially drawn map. The terrain involved can vary and the pace can be decided by the individual. It could be a family outing to the park or an international competition.

It's a versatile activity and can be done anywhere, from a dense forest to a playing field. This means that a course can be fixed or changed regularly, and difficulty levels can be changed to suit the people involved. All you need to get started is a sense of adventure, outdoor shoes and clothing, and, of course, a compass and map. There are various permanent courses around the country, or you could set up your own.

### Paragliding

Paragliding has developed as a more individual sport than parascending and usually takes place from suitable hillsides or mountains. Participants have to be able to walk up hills carrying the paraglider and its comfortable seat-shaped harness (in a huge back-pack). It's possible to have two-up air experience flights that don't require high levels of training or experience. Pilots have to be able to launch the canopy themselves, and quite some time is spent learning to do this successfully.

### Raft building

Raft building can be done on many levels, from producing a raft to carry a teddy bear across a paddling pool to a raft for carrying a whole patrol across a lake. It traditionally involves building a raft from various objects, usually pioneering poles, ropes and barrels. It's an activity that promotes teamwork and cooperation, and tests the group's knowledge of knots and their concept of building items from scratch.

### Sailing

The huge waves and icebergs of the southern ocean, as encountered by Ellen MacArthur in her round-the-world races, seem a very long way from the calm and glassy look of your local village pond. However, it's not as far removed as you might think.

Sailing is a sport that can be enjoyed by absolutely anyone. You needn't come from a sailing background, as there are plenty of places to learn the basics. You don't even need to own a boat, as clubs and centres will provide you with all you need to start: water, boat, buoyancy aid and the enthusiasum to have a go.

### Scuba diving

Scuba diving is underwater swimming with an air tank. The feeling of weightlessness and breathing underwater is both exhilarating and totally addictive. It can be done in most watery environments, from swimming pools to the Great Barrier Reef and all that goes between.

Scuba diving promotes non-verbal communication, increases self-confidence and allows people to try something new and exciting.

### Zorbing

Zorbing is a relatively new activity that evolved in New Zealand during the 1990s. It involves travelling inside a gigantic, bouncy, transparent PVC ball, surrounded by a thick cushion of air and another larger ball, the two balls being held together by hundreds of nylon threads. The zorb is pushed downhill, across a stretch of water or over the snow.

Zorbing can also be done with water inside the zorb, turning the experience into a wet and slippery one as you slide around. Up to three people can be put inside one zorb, which can reach speeds of up to 30mph.

A wide variety of sites across the UK offer zorbing. They're mainly open only during the summer months, but some stay open all year.

# SCOUTING FOR ALL

## Join the adventure

Scouting offers fun, challenge and everyday adventure to 400,000 girls and boys across the UK. We have a positive impact on the lives of young people, our adult volunteers and our local communities.

Offering over 200 different activities from abseiling and archery to drama, street sports and water zorbing, Scouting helps young people in the 6–25 age group grow in confidence, achieve their full potential and become active members of their communities.

This is only possible through the efforts of 100,000 volunteers who also enjoy the fun and friendship of Scouting. Trusted by nearly a million parents each week, the movement welcomes members from all backgrounds, faiths and cultures. Special emphasis is placed on bringing the Scouting programme to young people who currently do not benefit, particularly those in inner cities, those in rural areas and other disadvantaged groups.

The Scout Association is a registered charity in the UK and part of a worldwide movement of 31 million Scouts.

## Why volunteer?

Scouting is about fun and friendship for adults too. And with 30,000 young people still on our waiting lists there's no better time to get involved. You can give as much or as little time as you like and you can fit volunteering around your work and family commitments. Here's what you can expect:

- **Use your current skills and gain new ones**
- **Try new things and gain qualifications such as First Aid**
- **Become an active member of your community**
- **Meet new people and have fun**

We have opportunities:
- **to support young people**
- **in behind-the-scenes roles – from decorating a meeting place to driving the minibus**
- **to help lead our Groups, Districts, Counties and Regions as volunteer managers**